D1250491

LITURGIKON

LITURGIKON

Pastoral Ministrations

REV. WALTER J. SCHMITZ, S.S.
AND
REV. TERENCE E. TIERNEY

Our Sunday Visitor, Inc.
Noll Plaza, Huntington, Indiana 46750

Nihil Obstat:
Rev. Msgr. Joseph B. Coyne
Censor Deputatus

Imprimatur:
✠William Cardinal Baum
Archbishop of Washington
July 29, 1976

The Nihil Obstat and Imprimatur are official declarations that a book
or pamphlet is free of doctrinal or moral error. No implication is contained therein that those who have granted the Nihil Obstat and the
Imprimatur agree with the contents, opinions or statements expressed.

ISBN: 0-87973-894-4
Library of Congress Catalog Card Number: 77-76563

Cover Design by James E. McIlrath

First Printing, June 1977
Second Printing, November 1977
Third Printing, March 1978

Published, printed and bound in the U.S.A. by
Our Sunday Visitor, Inc.
Noll Plaza
Huntington, Indiana 46750

894

To our fellow priests
who cherish
what Vatican II's
Constitution on the Liturgy
has meant
liturgically and pastorally
in promoting
their priestly work
and dedication.

ACKNOWLEDGMENTS

The authors and publisher wish to thank all who have helped them prepare this pastoral handbook on the liturgy. Special thanks go to those who have given permission to use their materials in whole or in part; among them are the publishers, authors, editors, etc., whose copyrighted material appeared in the following:

New American Bible, ©1970 by the Confraternity of Christian Doctrine, Washington, D.C.

The Jerusalem Bible, ©1966 by Darton, Longman & Todd, Ltd., and Doubleday & Co., Inc., Garden City, New York.

Today's English Version of the New Testament, ©1966 and 1971 by the American Bible Society; published by The Macmillan Co., New York, New York.

"Catholics and the Bicentennial," National Conference of Catholic Bishops, Washington, D.C.

The Hospital Prayer Book, J. Massyngberde Ford, ©1975 by the Missionary Society of St. Paul the Apostle; published by Paulist Press, Paramus, New Jersey.

Prayers for the Dying, Bishop William G. Connare; published by the Priests of the Sacred Heart, Hales Corners, Wisconsin.

"Rite of Confirmation," Liturgical Commission, Diocese of Paterson, New Jersey.

"Liturgical Law," "Cremation," "New Rite of Penance" and "Public Celebration of Mass for Deceased Separated Christians" from *Emmanuel* magazine, Congregation of the Blessed Sacrament, New York, New York.

"Liturgical Celebrations: Patterns for Lent," James E. Dallen, North American Liturgy Resources, Cincinnati, Ohio.

English translation excerpts for the Rite of Marriage, the Rite of Burial and the Exposition of the Holy Eucharist, ©1969 and 1970 by the International Committee on English in the Liturgy, Inc., Washington, D.C.

TOPICAL TABLE OF CONTENTS

1 / Liturgical Law 13

2 / Liturgical and Pastoral Directives 17
   Mass Language 17
   Preaching 17
   Homily 17
   Homily — Sign of the Cross 18
   Role of the Deacon 18
   Altar 19
   Celebrant's Chair 19
   Lectern 19
   Reservation of the Eucharist 19
   Choir and Organ 19
   Adornment of the Altar 20
   Bread and Wine 20
   Sacred Vessels 20
   Communion Under Both Kinds 20
   Concelebration 21
   Bination on Weekdays 21
   All Souls' Day 21
   Trination 22
   Fulfilling Sunday Obligation on Saturday 22
   Mass in Homes 23
   Hour of Mass 23
   Eucharistic Fast 23
   Distribution of Holy Communion 24
   Celebration of Mass 24
   Stipends 24
   Missa Pro Populo 24
   Place of Mass 25
   Elderly and Infirm Priests 25
   Alcoholic Priests 25
   Time of Mass 25
   Admission of Other Christians to Eucharistic
      Communion in a Catholic Church 25

Oriental Catholics 27

Sacrament of Confirmation Administered by a Priest 27

Holy Thursday 28

Good Friday 28

Easter Vigil 28

Exposition of the Blessed Sacrament 29

Exposition for an Extended Period of Time 30

Extended Faculty for Receiving Holy Communion
    Twice on the Same Day 30

Rite of Reconciliation — Confessional Room 31

Final Antiphon of the Virgin Mary 31

Church Banners 31

Fast and Abstinence 32

Washing of Sacred Linens 32

Reception of Baptized Christians 32

Sacrament of the Anointing of the Sick 33

Receiving Holy Communion Twice on the Same Day 34

Extraordinary Ministers of the Eucharist 34

Funeral of Non-Catholics 35

Incensation 35

Incensation of the Altar 35

The Sign of Peace 36

3 / Celebration of Baptism 39

4 / Sacrament of Reconciliation 41

Proper Dress for Penance Rites 43

5 / Communal Penance 45

General Outline 45

Guidelines 45

Suggested Optional Texts for Communal Penance 46

Psalm 51 46

Service of Communal Penance 1 48

Service of Communal Penance 2 52

Marian Penance Service 58

Mary, Mother of the Redemption 65

Appendix of Scriptural Texts for Communal
    Penance Service 65
Courage Is for Forgiveness 71

6 / Sacrament of Confirmation 73
I. Introduction 73
Liturgical Reform 73
Dignity of Confirmation 73
Offices and Ministries in the Celebration
    of Confirmation 73
The Ceremony 73
II. Liturgical Considerations 74
III. Catechists 75
Significance of Roles 75
Significance of Material Signs 76
Methods Within the Classroom 76
IV. Notes for the Sacristan and Master of Ceremonies .. 77
V. The Commentator-Lector and Song Leader 77
VI. Order of the Rite of Confirmation 79
VII. The Rite of Confirmation Outside the Mass 84
Music Appendix 84

7 / Sacrament of Matrimony (With Appropriate Homilies) 87
Marriage Ceremony With Mass 87
Marriage Ceremony Without Mass 87
Suggested Reading Before the Marriage Ceremony 87
Exhortation Before the Sacrament of Matrimony 88
Wedding Homily 1 90
Wedding Homily 2 92
Wedding Homily 3 93
Wedding Homily 4 95
Celebration of a Wedding Anniversary 97
Renewal of the Marriage Vows 98
Rite for Celebrating Marriage During Mass 99
General Intercessions for the Marriage Ceremony 104
Suggested Prayer of Bride and Bridegroom After
    Holy Communion 113

Rite for Celebrating Marriage Outside Mass 114
Mixed Marriage Guidelines 119
Specific Norms 120

8 / Exposition of the Blessed Sacrament 125
Relationship Between Exposition and Mass 125
Regulations for Exposition 125
The Minister of Exposition 127
Rite of Eucharistic Exposition and Benediction 127
Hymns 130
Meditation 133
Prayers 133
Eucharistic Day or Holy Hour 136
Suggested Readings 136

9 / Prayers When Visiting the Sick 139
For Hospital Patients in General 139
For Patients With Eye Disorders 141
For Patients in Danger of Death 142
Traditional Prayers 143
Suggested Readings 144

10 / Rite of Anointing 145
A Pastoral Commentary 145
Guidelines for the Anointing of the Sick 148

11 / Prayers for the Dying 151
Recommendation of the Departing Soul to God 151

12 / Wake Services 159
A Celebration of Consolation: The Wake Service 159
Appendix of Scriptural Texts for Wake Service 164

13 / Christian Burial (With Appropriate Homilies) 171
Vigil Service on the Eve of Burial 171
Funeral Mass 174
Rite at the Entrance of the Church 174

General Funeral Homily 1 176

General Funeral Homily 2 177

Homily for Funerals 1 179

Homily for Funerals 2 180

Funeral Homily for a Public Servant 182

Funeral Homily for a Child 184

Funeral Homily for an Elderly Person 185

Public Celebration of Mass for Deceased
  Separated Christians 187

Final Commendation and Farewell When Celebrated
  in Church After Mass 190

Final Commendation and Farewell When Omitted
  in Church 199

14 / Cremation and Christian Burial 207

15 / Blessings for Persons, Places and Things 211

Blessing of Love (Attributed to St. Francis) 211

Prayers for Peace 212

Thanksgiving 212

For Our Fellowmen 213

Grace at Meals 214

Special Prayer for Thanksgiving Day 215

Wedding Banquet 215

For Our Enemies 215

For the Church 215

For Church Unity 216

For Our Country 216

For Civil Authorities 217

For Congress or a State Legislature 217

For Social Justice 218

For Those in the Armed Forces 218

Blessing of a School 219

For Schools and Colleges 219

Blessing for an Elderly Person 219

For the Sick 220

For One About to Undergo an Operation 220

For Childbirth 221

For the Poor and Neglected 221

For Those Who Mourn or Are Bereaved 221

Blessing in Time of Sorrow 222

For Families 222

Blessing of a House 223

Parental Blessing of a Child 224

For Guidance 224

All Souls' Day and Memorial Day 225

Blessing for a Good Harvest 225

Blessing of the Hunt 225

Blessing of Rosary Beads 226

Blessing of Articles of Devotion 226

A New Year's Blessing 227

For an Automobile (Or Any Other Kind of Vehicle) 227

For Travelers 227

Travelers' Blessing 228

For Safe Travel 228

For Any Special Need 229

Blessing for All Things 229

General Blessing 229

Prayer for Authorities (Traditionally Recited on
    Thanksgiving Day) 230

For Peace Among Nations 231

Index 233

1

Liturgical Law

One of the more difficult areas of law is that involving the regulation of the liturgy and the sacred minister or celebrant. This is because the law which regulates all aspects of liturgical celebration cannot be found in one source as, for instance, in the Code of Canon Law. To discover the norm for proper liturgical celebration one must turn to the introductory norms as contained in the liturgical books (e.g., the *General Instructions of the Roman Missal*) or the various instructional and Roman documents touching upon liturgy with a view to legislation. Because of this situation, liturgical law tends to become an amorphous mass of norms, many of which escape the minister's attention and at times prove pastorally harmful to the worshiping community. This condition is especially distressing when one considers that liturgical law is the most fundamental and proximate experience of law a priest or sacred minister confronts in his day-to-day ministry.

The 1917 Code of Canon Law does not deal explicitly with liturgical norm. In its section on general norms, under Canon II, it states: "The Code *as a rule* does not legislate regarding the rites and ceremonies which the liturgical books approved by the Latin Church prescribe for the celebration of the most holy sacrifice of the Mass, the administration of the sacraments and sacramentals, and other sacred functions." One can readily observe that, as far as liturgical law is concerned, the Code adopts a hands-off policy.

What is one to understand by this and what, *per se,* are the reasons for such a legal disclaimer, as viewed in Canon II? There are two reasons: (1) The peculiar character of liturgical law (that is, the nature of the law itself) works against its being included in codified legislation. The norms for divine worship are by their nature meticulous and ritualistic, thereby preventing their being included in a book of law. (2) The norms for celebration and otherwise pervasive liturgical regulations are so numerous that their inclusion in the Code of Canon Law would have rendered the Code too unwieldy. Hence, one finds the rules, norms and prescriptions not in a book of law but in general instructions on celebration and in each and every liturgical book itself. For example, the law governing the celebration of Mass can be found in the *General Instructions of the Roman Missal;* many other things relative to law can likewise be found in the Roman Missal. The laws governing the separate rites of baptism, anointing, confirmation, etc., can be found in the introductory section of each ritual book. Therefore, generally, the law regulating each sacrament is spelled out in the liturgical book or "ceremonial" of each individual sacrament.

13

Incidentally, here and there, the Code of Canon Law does legislate matters regarding rites and ceremonies; for example, in areas where doubts are to be resolved, defects supplied, certain changes specified. Illustration of these can be found in the Code under the section dealing with sacraments, sacred times and places, divine worship and sacramentals. These deal basically with diversity of rite, holy Mass and administration of sacraments. But the view is always to the canonical ordering of liturgy in a general way and not with a view to the legislating for specific sacramental celebration or regarding pre-Scripture rubrics. The Code would treat of liturgical matter *strictly,* not with liturgical matters which only touch upon discipline or celebration. Ergo, the liturgical law of the Church, properly so called, can be found in the official liturgical books which are approved by the Holy See or by the episcopal conferences insofar as the Vatican delegates this power to episcopal conferences in particular matters, e.g., Thanksgiving Day liturgy.

The usefulness of liturgical books is readily evident; not only do they provide the Church with proper format of sacramental celebration and the ordering of sacramental matter and form, but they provide the norms for proper regulation of worship with a view to sound ecclesial celebration. Without these norms the liturgy would become chaotic and unwieldy. Morever, the norms for worship insure that the unity of worship in a particular rite is maintained and safeguarded against unwarranted abuse. Since liturgy is a source, indeed, the font of unity, then the proper presentation of good sacramental order is essential to the Church's future and tradition. This in no way implies a uniformity (e.g., Latin was viewed in this light by many) but, on the contrary, fosters a unity of sacramental celebration which in turn builds up a unified faith community.

The norms of liturgy are not meant to be a means to insure monotonous worship but to assure the believing community of the Church that the essential aspects of their worship will be preserved as Christ had intended. The diversity of worship has long been recognized by the Church: to wit, the Eastern Rites. But this diversity is careful to maintain the unity in essentials which is needed for authentic gospel liturgy. Certain norms must be followed so as to protect the most sacred aspect of one's faith life from distortion at the hands of enthusiastic amateurs and reputable theologians alike.

Variety in liturgical celebration is greatly needed. No one doubts nor would argue this point. But the question of authentic and genuine liturgical adaptation must not descend into an awkward or unwieldy pastoral practice. One must continually guard against the temptation to usurp the venerable heritage of the Church in favor of some homespun variety of dubious value. Admittedly, occasions will arise when pastoral necessity will dictate one's deviating from the general liturgical norms of the Catholic Church; but this ought always to be the exception and not the rule.

The question of flexibility within the limits of law continues to be a pointed one, especially in modern times. The post-Vatican II experience has left the clergy with a great need to adapt to the unexpected situation as well as to the unforeseen demands emanating from the Church's program of renewal. These situations become somewhat critical when Church law and demands for good order conflict with particular circumstances and pastoral necessity. There is no easy avenue for relief. The resolution is mostly left to the priest's own good judgment.

In liturgical matters no sacred minister need fear gross reprisal from high churchmen for deviation in liturgical celebration so long as there exists a genuine need and a just cause. A priest or deacon should feel free to adapt the liturgy to the needs of the people whenever the situation calls for such action — but only when the need is legitimate. For example, it is one thing to use a special Eucharistic proper designed for children at a specifically children's liturgy (the Holy See has approved the use of three Eucharistic prayers called for by the National Conference of Catholic Bishops, or NCCB), and quite another thing altogether to employ unauthorized Eucharistic prayers at general parish Masses on Sunday morning, or on the occasion of some high Church feast.

To engage in enlightened adaptation, the sacred ministers must be apprised of what good liturgy is and how a variation can promote the good of souls under certain conditions. For a priest or deacon to alter seriously the character of liturgy as set by Rome and the NCCB, there should be present a real pastoral need, a just cause (e.g., *epikeia,* excusing causes, exempting causes, moral impossibility), and it ought to be directed toward a particular group or category of persons within the Church.

The liturgy is the efficacious point of contact between people and their God. It further represents the most profound area wherein people and law or authority converge. Apart from marriage law, people have their most intimate experience with Church law relative to liturgical celebration. Owing to this contact between law, people and liturgy, the Church rightly considers liturgical law to be most significant in the configuration of faith and order. Because of the impact of liturgical law on the Church, it forever remains a highly guarded area.

In a final note the priest should take particular interest in the distinction drawn between essential and accidental rubrics. An essential rubric is a norm of action which regulates, directs or otherwise orders a particularly significant aspect of sacramental liturgy with a view to insuring valid celebrations. The essential rubric touches upon the most profound element of liturgical activity. One should not casually approach an essential rubric or norm. (It should be understood that while the word "rubric" carries poor connotation today, it is really only a euphemism for a norm.) An accidental rubric is one which concerns aspects of liturgical celebration which are of lesser import and usually exist in order to promote fluid, artful and stately worship. These seldom touch upon the validity of a sacrament. Those rubrics or norms which usually appear in the front of the liturgical books (e.g., Roman Missal, Sacramentary, etc.) are generally of a more essential nature; those that appear throughout the text are generally accidental in nature.

This rule of thumb should be used when attempting to judge whether a norm or rubric is essential or accidental: Does this particular norm touch upon the essence of the sacrament? If the answer is yes, the norm is essential; otherwise it is accidental. (To wit: The rubric which states that the water used in baptism is to be poured in a flowing manner over the head of the one to be baptized, not sprinkled, is certainly more important than whether the mother or godmother holds the child.)

2

Liturgical and Pastoral Directives

In many instances, priests should consult their diocesan faculties over and above the general norms to assure that they are not violating regulations but acting in accord with the mind of the Church.

Only the Holy See may authorize experiments with the sacred liturgy. No individual priest or group of priests may experiment with the liturgy. "Therefore, absolutely no other person, not even a priest, may add, remove, or change anything in the liturgy on his own authority" (*Constitution on the Sacred Liturgy*, No. 22, Para. 3).

Mass Language

The English language in the celebration of the Mass is to be used. "In liturgical services which are celebrated in some places with people of another language, it is lawful, with the consent of the local ordinary, to use the vernacular known to those faithful, especially in the case of groups of immigrants, or of members of a personal parish, or similar instances" (Instruction dated September 26, 1964).

If, for sufficient reasons, some of the faithful should desire the celebration of Mass in Latin, such a Mass can be arranged. It is necessary that a Mass in Latin follow the new Roman Missal, approved by Pope Paul VI on April 3, 1969, and effective November 30, 1969.

The use of the Missal approved by Pius V is permitted only to priests for reasons of age or for other reasons approved by the ordinary. In such permissions this Missal may be used only at a Mass *sine populo*.

Preaching

Generally, priests should consult the chancery office for permission to speak on the radio or on television.

Interfaith talks should not be made without permission of the local chancery office or ecumenical commission.

Homily

The homily is strongly recommended as an integral part of the liturgy. It should develop some point of the readings or of another text from the Ordinary or the Mass of the day. A homily is prescribed for Sundays and holy days and highly recommended for other days, especially the weekdays of Advent and Lent as well as other occasions when there is a sizable group of people. Length and greatness are not synonymous in a daily homily. A simple thought, a few sentences to develop it, some scriptural ideas for the people to ponder and pray about during the day. When related to this Mass and this day, the homily can be well given in three minutes. It takes preparation. It is better to make one point well than to confuse everyone with a series of half-understood ideas. One's sense of pastoral needs will enable a priest to choose the point to be made, based on the liturgical maturity and the spiritual needs of the daily gathering of the faithful.

Homily — Sign of the Cross

Normally the homily is preached by the celebrant of the Mass and follows directly upon the proclamation of the gospel. The homily is considered to be a living explanation and an integral part of God's word and not an appendage or afterthought.

The use of the sign of the cross before the homily was never laid down as a rule. The present order of the Mass has one sign of the cross at the opening of the celebration and closes with the usual blessing.

The Sacred Congregation for the Sacraments and Divine Worship has approved the custom of *not* making the sign of the cross and has stated that the homily is *part* of the liturgy. Since the faithful have already made the sign of the cross at the beginning of the Mass, it is better that it should not be repeated before or after the homily.

Role of the Deacon

All deacons, including permanent deacons, may conduct the following rites: (a) administer baptism and supply the ceremonies that may have been omitted at baptism; (b) distribute Holy Communion at Mass and outside Mass; (c) conduct the rite of Viaticum; (d) impart benediction of the Blessed Sacrament to the faithful; (e) assist at marriages, but only in the parish to which he is assigned (before assisting at marriages his name must be registered with the city clerk or state office where such laws are in effect); (f) administer sacramentals; (g) preside at wake, funeral and burial rites; (h) proclaim the gospel, read the Scriptures, teach and preach to the faithful, preside over prayer meetings and Bible services.

A deacon may give all blessings contained in rites in which he is a minister, but for other rites he may not (e.g., blessing and distribution of ashes, blessing of rosaries and religious objects).

Altar

The Eucharist should be celebrated on an altar, either permanent (fixed) or movable. In places where Mass is not regularly offered, a suitable table may be used (e.g., home Masses). A consecrated altar stone or Greek corporal is not necessary for a movable altar, or on a table where the Eucharist is celebrated outside a sacred place. An altar cloth and a corporal must always be supplied.

Celebrant's Chair

The celebrant's chair indicates his office of presiding over the assembly and directing prayer. Hence the proper place for the celebrant's chair is in the center of the sanctuary, facing the congregation. If the sanctuary arrangement prevents this, it may be placed to the side of the sanctuary, but must nevertheless be facing the people.

Lectern

"Ordinarily the lectern or ambo should be a fixed pulpit and not a simple movable stand. Depending on the structure of the church, it should be so placed that the ministers may be easily seen and heard by the faithful. The readings, responsorial psalm and *Exultet* are proclaimed from the lectern. It may be used also for the homily and intercessions (prayers of the faithful). It is less suitable for the commentator, cantor or choirmaster to use the lectern" (*General Instructions of the Roman Missal,* No. 272, Paras. 2, 3, 4).

Reservation of the Eucharist

"It is highly recommended that the Holy Eucharist be reserved in a chapel suitable for private adoration and prayer. If this is impossible because of the structure of the church or local custom, it should be kept on an altar or other place in the church that is prominent and properly decorated" (*General Instructions of the Roman Missal,* No. 276).

Choir and Organ

Since the choir forms part of the assembly of the faithful, it should be so located that it exercises its function of full sacramental participation. The organ and other approved musical instruments (e.g., guitars at folk Mass celebrations) should be located in a suitable place so that they may properly assist both the choir and the congregation.

Adornment of the Altar

Candles are required for liturgical services. They should be placed on the altar or around it, in harmony with the structure of the altar and the sanctuary. The candles should not obstruct the view of the ceremony at the altar. Flowers may be placed near the altar, but not on the altar and again not in great profusion. The number of candles and the amount of flowers must be in good taste and express the degree of festivity.

Bread and Wine

According to Church tradition the bread must be made from wheat and must be unleavened. The wine for the Eucharist must be natural and pure and not mixed with any foreign substance. Various types of wine (e.g., rosé, white, red, etc.) are supplied by approved dealers. These wines are approved for sacramental purposes as long as the alcoholic content does not exceed the regulation of twelve percent established by the Sacred Congregation for the Sacraments and Divine Worship.

Sacred Vessels

The chalice and paten should be made from solid materials, but not from absorbent material. Materials which are considered precious and valuable and at the same time appropriate may be used for sacred vessels. It is suitable to use one large paten for the consecration of the bread for the celebrant and the faithful. Vessels made from metal which oxidize should ordinarily be gilded on the inside; if the metal is precious and does not oxidize, gilding is not necessary. "The artist may give a form to the vessels, which is in keeping with the culture of the area and their purpose in the liturgy" (*General Instructions of the Roman Missal,* No. 295).

Communion Under Both Kinds

(a) The communicant approaches the altar and receives the sacred host from the celebrant while he says, "The body of Christ." The communicant answers, "Amen." If there is a deacon to assist the celebrant, the communicant receives from the chalice, answering "Amen" as the deacon says, "The blood of Christ." (b) If there is no deacon to assist, the celebrant holds the chalice while each communicant receives the consecrated wine, but only after all have already received the sacred host. The same prayers are recited and the communicants do not hold the chalice as they receive. A purificator is provided for the communicants to guard against the spilling of the precious blood. (c) *Communion by intinction.* If there is a deacon or an acolyte to assist at Communion time, the celebrant dips the particle into the chalice and says, "The body and blood of Christ" — to which the communicant responds, "Amen." There is no special problem when the celebrant uses the combination Communion dish to which a small chalice is attached for the convenience of Communion under both kinds by intinction.

Concelebration

General Instruction No. 153 of the Roman Missal states that concelebration is allowed "with the permission of the ordinary, who may decide whether concelebration is suitable . . . when the needs of the faithful do not require that all priests present celebrate individually at any kind of meeting of priests. . . ." Most dioceses permit concelebration at funerals of priests and laymen, weddings and various ecclesiastical functions. The principal celebrant always wears the chasuble; concelebrants do likewise, except when there is an insufficiency of vestments. The concelebrants may omit the chasuble but wear the stole over the alb. The amice may be omitted, provided the alb fits properly around the neck, so as not to give an unkempt appearance. The concelebrants receive from the chalice at the altar immediately after they receive the sacred host.

Bination on Weekdays

Pastorale Munus permits the faculty of celebrating holy Mass twice on weekdays when additional priests are not available, e.g., funeral or nuptial Masses or to fulfill the parochial Mass schedule. Many dioceses permit priests to invoke this privilege of bination for the purpose of offering home Masses. In these cases the celebrant may accept only one stipend unless diocesan regulations allow a second stipend for a particular purpose designated by the ordinary.

All Souls' Day

Normally on All Souls' Day the directives of the Ordo are followed. However, should All Souls' Day occur on Sunday the feast is not transferred to the following day. The Masses prescribed for All Souls' Day are celebrated on Sunday displacing the Sunday scheduled Mass.

White, violet or black vestments may be worn for these Masses. The Gloria, Credo and one of the prefaces for the dead are recited. The readings from the Liturgy of the Hours (Divine Office) are those specified for that particular Sunday. The Mass for the particular Sunday is celebrated on the first free ferial day of the current week.

A priest is free to offer three Masses on November 2. He may apply one of these Masses for anyone he wishes and in return for a stipend; he may not, however, accept a stipend for either of the other two, which he must respectively apply for all the faithful departed and for the intention of the Holy Father.

A priest is not obliged to say the three Masses permitted on November 2. If he says one Mass only, he shall celebrate the first of the three Masses; this he may apply for whatever intention he wishes and in return accept a stipend. If he celebrates only two Masses, he shall say the first and second Masses as listed in the Missal. He may apply one of these two Masses for whatever intention he wishes and likewise accept a stipend, but not for the second Mass which he must apply for the faithful departed.

Trination

Pastorale Munus states that if true necessity demands, the faculty of celebrating three Masses on Sundays and holy days of obligation is permitted. The motive for this is that genuine care of souls is necessary. This privilege may be used as often as this might seem necessary in order to maintain the regular schedule of Masses for the public good on Sundays and days of precept. The celebrant of three Masses accepts only one stipend; those obliged to celebrate the Mass *pro populo* may not accept a stipend at all.

Celebration of Mass on the vigil of Easter (Holy Saturday) does not prevent one from binating on Easter Sunday, if necessity demands. The same privilege holds when one offers Mass on Saturday evening or the eve of a holy day.

Fulfilling Sunday Obligation on Saturday

The Instruction on Eucharistic Worship (May 25, 1967) by the Sacred Congregation of Rites as well as the Instruction of the Sacred Congregation for the Clergy (January 10, 1970) grant the faculty for the faithful to fulfill their Sunday or holy day of obligation on the previous evening. The documents state that the faithful should be properly instructed and that this permission in no way is intended to diminish or obscure the position of Sunday in our Eucharistic worship. This privilege is granted for the convenience of people and their Sunday obligation.

In many dioceses this permission is limited to one or, at most, two evening Masses with the stipulation that those Masses are not to begin earlier than 5:00 p.m. Some dioceses direct that a nuptial Mass on Saturday evening at five o'clock or later does not satisfy the Sunday obligation.

The proper evening Mass (on Saturday or before a holy day) is the Mass assigned to the Sunday or holy day.

The faithful who attend the evening Mass may receive Holy Communion even if they have already received Holy Communion in the morning.

When a holy day falls on a Saturday or Monday there are *two* obligations to fulfill: one for the holy day and one for the Sunday. The obligation for each day can be observed by attendance at Mass on the evening before or on the day itself.

Mass in Homes

The faculty of offering holy Mass in the homes of parishioners is in accord with *Pastorale Munus* and the Bishops' Commission on Liturgy. The gathering should be restricted to a relatively small number, the purpose being to form a group with a genuine sense of community. This privilege *can be used only on weekdays,* and all liturgical prescriptions must be observed. A homily should be given. Many dioceses permit the pastor to invoke the faculty of bination for the purpose of offering a home Mass since this is a parochial Mass.

Home Masses may *not* be celebrated on Sundays and other days of precept. (*Note:* Normally, vestments worn at church Masses are used at home Masses; white supplies for all colors.)

Hour of Mass

Pastorale Munus grants the privilege of celebrating Mass for a reasonable cause at any hour of the day.

Nuptial Masses may be celebrated in the afternoon or evening, but the exercise of this faculty is left to the judgment of the pastor. It is the right of the pastor to establish reasonable regulations about the hours for weddings, so as not to conflict with other parochial functions.

Eucharistic Fast

There must be one hour of abstention from solid food and liquids (except water which never breaks the fast) before the moment of Holy Communion. This applies to the celebrant of the Mass as well as to the laity (cf. *De Sacra Communione et de Cultu Mysterii Eucharistici extra Missam*).

Many canonists state that this faculty extends expressly to the interval between one Mass and another; some few canonists apply the faculty to *either* of the bination Masses or before any of the trination Masses. This privilege is applicable at bination Masses both on Sundays and on weekdays (cf. *Pastorale Munus* with the ordinary's permission).

The Eucharistic fast for the sick and the elderly is reduced to fifteen minutes and applies also to those caring for them.

Distribution of Holy Communion

Holy Communion may be given to the sick *at any hour*. The Roman Missal provides that on Good Friday, Holy Communion may be brought *at any hour* to the sick who cannot participate in the prescribed liturgical services. This does not apply on Holy Saturday except by way of Viaticum.

When Holy Communion is distributed in a parish church outside Mass under usual circumstances, *Pastorale Munus* specifies that there must be a brief celebration, which consists of a short homily or readings, hymns and concluding with a prayer of the faithful and the Lord's Prayer.

Celebration of Mass

Normally special permission should be obtained for the celebration of Mass in the open air or in a public building for some extraordinary occasion. Permission for home Masses has been granted generally by local ordinaries.

Stipends

Diocesan regulations should be consulted about stipends for various functions, e.g., weddings, funerals, bination or trination. In many instances all stipends or stole fees are given over for the maintenance of the church and not retained by the individual priest. If a stipend is allowed for bination or trination on Sundays, the ordinary may designate a particular fund.

Missa Pro Populo

A pastor or an administrator of a parish is obliged to celebrate Mass for his people every Sunday of the year and the prescribed holy days. If one of these feasts falls on a Sunday one Mass fulfills the obligation.

Place of Mass

The Eucharist (Mass) should normally be celebrated in a sacred place on a permanent or movable altar. Outside a sacred place, especially if *ad modum actus,* it can be celebrated on any suitable table, always keeping the altar cloth and corporal.

Elderly and Infirm Priests

Permission to offer Mass *habitually* in the home, to offer special votive Masses *only,* or for infirm priests to offer Mass while seated may be obtained from the chancery. Elderly priests who find it difficult to celebrate Mass according to the new Roman Missal may seek permission to celebrate according to the older Roman Missal, but such celebrations cannot take place publicly.

Alcoholic Priests

Only the ordinary of a diocese may grant an alcoholic priest, upon his personal request, offering a concelebrated Mass, permission to receive the Eucharist under only the species of bread, or when a concelebrated Mass is not possible, to use unfermented grape juice (pure grape juice containing no additives) instead of wine. This permission applies only to priests who are undergoing or have undergone treatment for alcoholism. One must avoid creating scandal to the faithful.

Time of Mass

Pastorale Munus grants the faculty to celebrate Mass, for a just cause, at any hour of the day, and to distribute Holy Communion in the evening, with due observances of the other requirements of the law. The exercise of this faculty depends on the prudent judgment of the pastor and for the common good of his subjects.

Admission of Other Christians to Eucharistic Communion in a Catholic Church

• *Two Doctrinal Principles Concern the Eucharist*

1. The Eucharist is very much linked to the *mystery of the Church:* (a) since the Eucharist is a sign of the unity of the Church; (b) since the local celebration of the Eucharist is a profession in the

whole Church; (c) because this sacramental ministry is always held in communion with the Pope and bishops.

2. On the other hand, however, the Eucharist is *a spiritual food,* which is necessary to every Christian.

• *Two Principles Govern Admission to the Eucharist*

1. The strict relationship between the mystery of the Church and the mystery of the Eucharist can never be altered.

2. The principle of the relationship between the Church and the Eucharist will not be obscured if the Christian admitted to Holy Communion: (a) has a faith in the sacrament in conformity with that of the Church; (b) experiences a serious spiritual need for the Eucharistic sustenance; (c) is unable for a long period of time to have recourse to a minister of his own community; (d) asks for the sacrament of his own accord; (e) has the proper dispositions and leads a life worthy of a Christian.

Besides these conditions, the admission of these other Christians to Holy Communion should not endanger or disturb the faith of Catholics.

• *Practical Application of These Principles*

1. Intercommunion with the separated Eastern Churches is governed by the Second Vatican Council's *Decree on the Eastern Catholic Churches.*

2. Since our ties with Protestant Christians are not as close as with the Orthodox, admission of Protestant Christians to the Eucharist can take place only in exceptional cases of urgent necessity. The 1967 Directory mentioned three cases of urgent necessity as follows: (a) danger of death; (b) people suffering persecution; (c) people in prison.

3. This instruction says that besides these three cases, a Christian might find he is in grave spiritual necessity if he is deprived of the Eucharist over a period of time, because of the great trouble and expense which he would have to undergo to contact his own religious community. Permission would have to be *obtained from the local ordinary* in each particular case.

POSSIBLE CASES — (1) *Catholics receiving Holy Communion in Orthodox Churches:* This is governed by the conciliar decree on the Eastern Churches; however, the Orthodox bishops of America have not accepted the practice of intercommunion. Since this is so, their desires should be acceded to. (2) *Catholics receiving Communion in Protestant Churches:* This is not permitted on any occasion even by the new instruction. (3) *Orthodox receiving Holy Communion in the Catholic Church:* This, too, is governed by the decree on Eastern Churches; however, again, the Orthodox hierarchy of America has said that this should not be done. (4) *Protestants receiving Holy Communion in the Catholic Church:* Refer to the foregoing explanations.

It must be stressed that if a priest feels that a Protestant within his parish qualifies for intercommunion under the above guidelines, he should petition the chancery. The document does not allow the distribution of Holy Communion to non-Catholics on the occasion of weddings, funerals or other similar services.

Oriental Catholics

Normally, Oriental Catholics are to be cared for by the clergy of their own rite. If they do not have their own clergy, they are cared for by the local Latin Rite parish. This is to assure the validity of marriages, but it does not in any way imply a change of rite. Children belong to the jurisdiction of that pastor to whose rite their father belongs.

Children must be baptized in the rite of their parents, or in cases of mixed Catholic rites, in the rite of their father. If for any reason the child is not baptized in his proper rite, he still belongs to his proper rite and is obliged by Canon Law of that rite. Since most Oriental Catholics are confirmed at baptism, care should be taken on the occasion of confirmation in the parish that these children are not confirmed again.

Marriages of Catholics of mixed rites should take place in the rite of the groom. The chancery office, under certain circumstances, can make an exception and allow the marriage to take place in the rite of the bride. *In all cases of marriage regarding Oriental Catholics,* even those who do not have their proper ordinary, whether marrying among themselves or with a Latin Catholic, priests should check with the chancery to be certain that the Canon Law is observed.

Sacrament of Confirmation Administered by a Priest

Ordinarily the sacrament of confirmation is administered by the bishop. In addition to the bishop the law gives the faculty to confirm to the following: (a) priests who, in virtue of an office which they lawfully hold, baptize an adult or a child old enough for catechesis, or admit a validly baptized adult into full communion with the Church; (b) in cases where there is danger of death, provided a bishop is not easily available or is lawfully impeded: pastors and parochial vicars; in their absence, their parochial associates; priests who are in charge of special parishes lawfully established; administrators, substitutes and assistants; in the absence of all of the preceding, any priest who is not subject to censure or canonical penalty; (c) in case of a large number of persons to be confirmed, the bishop may designate in the administration of the sacrament the pastors of the places where the candidates belong, or priests who have taken a special part in the preparation of the candidates.

When a priest confers the sacrament under these circumstances an entry of confirmation should be made in the parochial register, e.g., "Danger of death — no bishop available."

Holy Thursday

Most dioceses grant permission for only one Mass in the morning hours, a Mass of accommodation. All private Masses are forbidden, since it is fitting that the clergy concelebrate at the principal Mass. The Holy Thursday rubrics read: "For pastoral reasons the local ordinary may permit on Holy Thursday another Mass to be celebrated in churches and public oratories or semi-public oratories in the evening, and in the case of genuine necessity, also in the morning, but only for those who are in no way able to take part in the evening Mass. The two additional Masses must not be celebrated for the advantage of private persons or prejudice the principal evening Mass."

To demonstrate the unity of the priesthood, priests should concelebrate on Holy Thursday at the Mass of Chrism. Concelebration at the Chrism Mass does not prohibit a priest from celebrating or concelebrating at a parish evening Mass.

On Holy Thursday a priest: (a) may concelebrate at the Mass of the Chrism; (b) concelebrate the solemn evening parish Mass; (c) celebrate, if necessary, another Mass which is required for the needs of the faithful.

Good Friday

The Sacred Congregation for the Sacraments and Divine Worship has granted to American bishops permission to repeat the solemn liturgical functions "if the size or nature of a parish or other community indicates the pastoral need for an additional liturgical service on Good Friday." This determination must be made in the best interests of the parish by the pastor.

Holy Communion may be given to the faithful *only* at the celebration of the Lord's Passion but not at ceremonies like the Way of the Cross. Holy Communion may be brought to the sick who cannot participate in the ceremonies, and this at any hour of the day.

Easter Vigil

The Sacred Congregation for the Sacraments and Divine Worship has granted permission to the American bishops to allow an additional Mass on the vigil for pastoral reasons as an anticipated Mass of Easter

Sunday provided that this additional celebration takes place *after* the celebration of the Easter vigil.

The new Roman Missal states that the celebration of the Easter vigil should take place during the night, so that it does not start before nightfall and should be finished by daylight of Easter. The sense of the rubrics seems to be that it should not be celebrated if it is light outside. The original Latin *nocte* certainly indicates darkness rather than twilight or early dawn. This would permit the Easter vigil Mass about 6:30 or 7:00 p.m. and would permit another Mass at 8:30 or 9:00 (as an anticipated Mass of Easter Sunday if pastoral reasons seem to warrant it).

Exposition of the Blessed Sacrament

Exposition of the Blessed Sacrament, whether in a pyx or monstrance, is a recognition of the wondrous presence of Christ in the sacrament and stimulates us to unite ourselves to him in a spiritual union which finds its culmination in sacramental Communion. Accordingly, it is eminently in harmony with the worship we owe him in spirit and in truth. Care must be taken that in exposition the worship of the Blessed Sacrament should clearly express its relation to the Mass. In the arrangements of exposition everything should be carefully excluded which might in any way obscure the intention of Christ who instituted the Eucharist primarily in order to make himself available to us as food, as healing and as consolation.

Exposition of the Blessed Sacrament merely for the purpose of giving benediction is forbidden. Devotion, both private and public, toward the Blessed Sacrament is highly recommended since the Eucharistic sacrifice is the source and summit of the entire Christian life. Regulations of the Second Vatican Council, as well as the relationship to be maintained between the liturgy and other nonliturgical celebrations, must be kept in mind. Especially important is the regulation which states: "The liturgical seasons must be taken into account, and these devotions must harmonize with the liturgy, be in some way derived from it and lead the people toward the liturgy as something which of its nature is far superior to these devotions."

While the Blessed Sacrament is exposed, the celebration of Mass in the same part of the church is forbidden. If exposition is prolonged for a day or for a number of successive days it should be interrupted during the celebration of Mass, unless Mass is celebrated in a chapel apart from the exposition and some of the faithful remain in adoration.

Genuflection on one knee is prescribed before the Blessed Sacrament whether it be reserved in the tabernacle or exposed for public adoration.

For exposition of the Blessed Sacrament in the monstrance, four or six candles should be lighted, that is, as many as are used at Mass, and incense should be used. For exposition in the pyx only, two candles should be lighted; incense may also be used.

Exposition for an Extended Period of Time

In churches in which the Blessed Sacrament is habitually reserved, it is recommended that there be a period of solemn exposition of the Blessed Sacrament every year, even though it may not be entirely continuous, so that the local community may have the opportunity to meditate on the Blessed Sacrament and adore it more fervently.

Where continuous adoration is not possible because there is not a sufficient number of the faithful available for adoration, it is permissible to replace the Blessed Sacrament in the tabernacle at times which have been arranged and duly announced. This may be done not more than twice in the day — for example, at midday and at night.

The replacing of the Blessed Sacrament may be done without undue ceremony. A priest or deacon wearing an alb or surplice and stole over his cassock, having adored the Blessed Sacrament for a brief period and having recited a prayer with the faithful, places the Blessed Sacrament in the tabernacle. It will be exposed again in the same manner at the hour appointed.

Extended Faculty for Receiving
Holy Communion Twice on the Same Day

"According to the discipline currently in force, the faithful are permitted to receive Holy Communion a second time on a given day. Special circumstances can occur when the faithful who have already received Holy Communion that same day, or even priests who have already celebrated Mass, may be present at some community celebration. They may receive Holy Communion again in the following instances: (a) at those Masses in which the sacraments of baptism, confirmation, anointing of the sick, sacred orders and matrimony are administered; also at a Mass at which First Communion is received; (b) at Masses at which a church or altar is consecrated; at Masses of religious profession or for the conferring of a 'canonical mission'; (c) at the following Masses of the dead: the funeral Mass, the Mass celebrated after the notification of death, the Mass on the day of final burial and the Mass on the first anniversary; (d) at the principal Mass celebrated in the cathedral or in the parish on the feast of Corpus Christi and on the day of a parochial visitation; at the Mass celebrated by the major superior of a religious community on the occasion of a canonical visitation, of special meetings or chapters; (e) at the principal Mass of a Eucharistic or Marian Congress, whether international or national, regional or diocesan; (f) at the principal Mass of any congress, sacred pilgrimage or preaching mission for the people; (g) in the administration of Viaticum, in which Communion can also be given to the relatives and friends of the patient; (h) also, local ordinaries may, besides these cases mentioned above, grant permission *ad actum* to receive Holy Communion twice on the same day, as often as they shall judge it truly justified by reason of genuinely special circumstances, according to the norm of this instruction" (*Immensae Caritatis,* January 28, 1973).

Rite of Reconciliation — Confessional Room

The American bishops have approved the idea that small chapels or rooms of reconciliation are highly desirable, in which penitents might choose to confess their sins and seek sacramental reconciliation through an informal face-to-face exchange with the priest and also appropriate counsel. Such chapels or rooms should be designed to afford the penitent the option of kneeling at a fixed confessional grille or priedieu in the customary way, but in every case the freedom of the penitent should be respected.

Final Antiphon of the Virgin Mary

When completing the daily recitation of the Liturgy of the Hours, one is free to recite any one of the antiphons of the Blessed Virgin, except the "Regina Coeli" ("Queen of Heaven"), which is strictly reserved for the Easter season. Likewise one is not necessarily bound to recite the Compline (or Night Prayer) before midnight. It is strictly a "night prayer" to be recited upon retiring for the evening.

Church Banners

Banners are permitted and must contribute visibility to the whole environment and the whole action. They are not self-contained, but they must speak to the faithful and give a new meaning to a familiar ritual and season or feast or setting in the place of worship.

Banners can speak and give meaning: they communicate like silent voices. They are able to express love and concern, grace and thoughtfulness, or the opposite kinds of sentiments. Banners can speak in various ways, but are particularly expressive in the use of symbol, since design is very important. Their design ought to have meaningful, functional, basic forms of extreme purity and simplicity that serve worship without contrivance. Banners should and must move the faithful to deeper participation. Their warmth, color, design and placement in church speak to the occasion. The guiding principle for good, meaningful banners is simplicity which provides a genuine richness of expression.

Lenten Fast and Abstinence

The National Conference of Catholic Bishops issued the following pastoral statement for Lenten regulations:

ABSTINENCE — The Fridays of Lent and Ash Wednesday. Everyone from the fourteenth birthday exclusive is bound to observe the law of abstinence.

FAST AND ABSTINENCE — Ash Wednesday and Good Friday. Everyone from the twenty-first birthday exclusive to the fifty-ninth birthday inclusive is bound to observe the law of fast.

The practice of granting dispensations from the law of fast and abstinence is no longer necessary. It is left to the *individual's conscience* to determine whether there is sufficient reason to excuse oneself from fast and abstinence on the days when they oblige. The bishops have stated: "No Catholic Christian will *lightly* excuse himself from so hallowed an obligation on the Wednesday which solemnly opens the Lenten season and on that Friday called Good Friday because on that day Christ suffered in the flesh and died for our sins." To reiterate, the bishops have expressed confidence that "no Catholic Christian will *lightly* hold himself excused from this penitential practice."

The bishops further strongly recommend participation in daily Mass and some self-imposed observance of fasting for all other weekdays of Lent.

Washing of Sacred Linens

Pastorale Munus now permits the *first* washing of sacred linens (palls, corporals and purificators) which have been used in the sacrifice of the Mass to be done by others than clerics. This permission is extended to lay religious as well as women.

Reception of Baptized Christians

1. The rite of reception of one born and baptized in a separated ecclesial community into full communion with the Catholic Church, according to the Roman or Latin Rite, is to be arranged without any great burden or inconvenience to the recipient.

2. Eastern Christians are required to make only a profession of faith, even if they are permitted with an apostolic indult to transfer to the Latin Rite.

3. The rite should generally be celebrated within Mass so that the recipient will receive Holy Communion.

4. No abjuration of heresy is required for one born and baptized outside the communion of the Catholic Church; the only requirement is the profession of faith.

5. The sacrament of baptism may not be repeated and conditional baptism is not permitted unless there is a reasonable doubt about the fact or validity of the baptism already received.

6. If the profession of faith and reception take place within Mass, the one to be received, depending on his personal dispositions, should confess his sins. He should first inform the confessor that he is about to be received into full communion.

7. The candidate should be accompanied if possible by a sponsor, preferably the man or woman who has the chief part in bringing him to full communion or in preparing the candidate. Two sponsors are permitted.

8. Holy Communion may be received under both species not only by the candidate but also by his sponsors, parents and spouse, if they are Catholics; also by lay catechists who have given instructions and also by all Catholics present, if the numbers or other circumstances suggest this.

Sacrament of the Anointing of the Sick

1. The sacrament of the anointing of the sick is administered to those who are dangerously ill, by anointing them on the forehead and hands with properly blessed olive oil or, if opportune, with another vegetable oil and saying, *once only,* the following words: "Through this holy anointing may the Lord in his love and mercy help you with the grace of the Holy Spirit. R. Amen. May the Lord who frees you from sin save you and raise you up. R. Amen."

2. In case of necessity, however, it is sufficient that a single anointing — the whole formula being pronounced — be given on the forehead or, because of the particular condition of the sick person, another more suitable part of the body.

3. This sacrament can be repeated if the sick person, having received the anointing, recovers and then again falls ill or if, in the course of the same illness, the danger becomes more serious.

4. *Confirmation.* Most dioceses grant permission to priests, even curates, to administer the sacrament of confirmation to persons in danger of death, in those parishes which are responsible for hospitals. The decree granting this power to curates speaks in terms of the pastor being absent which can be interpreted in the broadest sense. The sacra-

ment of confirmation should be given even to those who have not reached the age of reason. Therefore, a priest who baptizes in danger of death would also have a serious obligation to confirm the child at the same time.

Receiving Holy Communion
Twice on the Same Day

The privilege of receiving Holy Communion twice on the same day is granted on the following occasions:

1. On the evening of Saturday or of the day preceding a holy day of obligation, when the recipients intend to fulfill the precept of hearing Mass, even though they have already received Holy Communion on the morning of that same day.

2. At the second Mass of Easter and at one of the Masses celebrated on Christmas Day, even if the recipients have already received Holy Communion at the Mass of the Paschal Vigil or at the midnight Mass of Christmas.

3. At the evening Mass of Holy Thursday, even if the recipients have received Holy Communion at the earlier Mass of the Chrism.

4. *Special Circumstances.* (a) If Holy Communion has already been received at an earlier Mass, it can be received again at a Mass where the sacraments of baptism, confirmation, anointing of the sick, sacred orders and matrimony are administered; also at a Mass at which First Communion is received. (b) In the administration of Viaticum, in which Holy Communion can be given to the relatives and friends of the patient. (c) Local ordinaries may grant permission *ad actum* to receive Holy Communion twice on the same day, as often as they shall judge it truly justified by reasons of genuinely special circumstances.

Extraordinary Ministers of the Eucharist

1. Local ordinaries have the faculty to permit a suitable person individually chosen as an extraordinary minister for a specific occasion, or for a time, or in the case of necessity, in some permanent way to give the Eucharist to himself or to other faithful and to take it to the sick who are confined to their homes. This faculty may be used whenever: (a) there is no priest, deacon or acolyte; (b) the number of faithful requesting Holy Communion is such that the celebration of Mass or the distribution of the Eucharist outside of Mass would be unduly prolonged.

2. Local ordinaries have the faculty to permit individual priests exercising their sacred office to appoint a suitable person who in case of

genuine necessity would distribute Holy Communion for a specific occasion.

3. The person who has been appointed to be an extraordinary minister of Holy Communion is necessarily to be duly instructed and should distinguish himself by his Christian life, faith and morals. Let him strive to be worthy of this great office; let him cultivate devotion to the Holy Eucharist and show himself as an example to the other faithful by his piety and reverence for this most holy sacrament of the altar. Care should be taken that no one be chosen whose selection may cause scandal among the faithful.

4. Extraordinary ministers of the Eucharist distribute Holy Communion according to the liturgical norms.

Funeral of Non-Catholics

The funeral Mass may not be celebrated for the burial of a non-Catholic. In such circumstances the Liturgy of the Word may be celebrated in the church with the body present, and Holy Communion may be given to all not prevented from sharing in the Eucharist according to the established norms.

The prayers and readings recommended for wake services may be used in these cases. For the interment services, the prayers should ordinarily be taken from the ritual.

(See also "Public Celebration of Mass for Deceased Separated Christians," in Chapter 13 of this book.)

Incensation

The use of incense is optional in any form of Mass: (a) during the entrance procession; (b) at the beginning of Mass, to incense the altar; (c) at the procession and proclamation of the gospel; (d) at the offertory, to incense the offerings, altar, priest and people; (e) at the elevation of the host and chalice after the consecration.

Incensation of the Altar

The priest puts incense into the censer and blesses it silently with the sign of the cross. The altar is incensed in this manner: (a) if the altar is freestanding, the priest incenses it as he walks around it; (b) if the altar is attached to the wall, he incenses it while walking first to the right side, then to the left side.

If there is a cross on the altar or near it, the priest incenses it before he incenses the altar. If the cross is behind the altar, the priest incenses it when he passes in front of it.

Funeral Mass: If incense is used, the priest, after incensing the gifts and the altar, may incense the body. The deacon or another minister then incenses the priest and people.

The Sign of Peace

The reintroduction of the kiss of peace (or *pax*) within the Mass was not perhaps preceded by sufficient catechesis covering its history, significance and use. In the Roman tradition the sign of peace which initially concluded the celebration of the Liturgy of the Word, seemed to be drawn always into the Liturgy of the Eucharist itself. First, it was introduced as a prelude to the offering of the gifts, then as the conclusion of the Eucharistic prayer, and finally, especially after St. Gregory the Great, as a natural and useful extension of the Lord's Prayer in preparation for Holy Communion.

With regard to the sharing of the sign of peace, from *Ordo Romanus I* and the other *ordines* it appears that the *pax* did not start from the celebrant but with each member of the clergy exchanging it with his neighbor and the faithful among themselves. Furthermore, Andrieu's *Capitulare Ecclesiastici Ordinis* expressly states that once the priest has said, "Pax Domini," and all have responded with the words, "Et cum spiritu tuo," "immediately . . . the clerics and people offer the sign of peace among themselves where they are standing." There is no moving around and no disturbance; each offers the sign of peace with the person nearest to him or her.

Whereas the first Roman Ordo states that at the given signal, those in the nave of the church greeted each other with the kiss, later manuscripts of this Ordo introduced an inconspicuous but important change. The kiss of peace is made to proceed from the altar and, like a message or gift, is handed on "to the others and to the people." With this in view it was only natural that the kiss of peace would no longer come from the deacon but from the celebrant as if from Christ himself. Thus, the celebrant was first to kiss the altar or according to other sources, the Missal, crucifix, chalice, or the consecrated gifts before offering the sign of peace to the others.

This solution reflects rather well the tendency and the mentality of the Middle Ages — a mentality which clericalized everything in the liturgy. The assembly of the faithful, always clearly distinct and separate, was to be content with watching, assisting and receiving. The kiss of peace was also to be received from a cleric.

The liturgical renewal has recognized the value of the assembly and its right to participate actively in the liturgy. The *Constitution on the Sacred Liturgy,* No. 7, in indicating the various forms of the real presence of Christ, emphasized his presence in the assembly itself.

In view of this providential reevaluation of the liturgical assembly, it is proper therefore that in the *General Instructions of the Roman*

Missal, No. 112, and in the order of the Mass, it is clearly stated that at the invitation addressed to the faithful all exchange the sign of peace according to local custom. It is not a peace that moves out from the altar, a clericalized peace, but a community peace exchanged among those in whose midst is the real presence of Christ the Lord.

The practice where the priest moves out into the nave of the church, among the faithful, to offer personally to them the *pax* is basically a return to the clericalism of the past, oblivious of the reality of the liturgical assembly.

Thus the priest need not move from the altar to offer the sign of peace to this or that person. This is clearly deduced from the *ordo Missae* itself which indicates that after the deacon or priest states, "Let us offer each other the sign of peace," and "all make an appropriate sign of peace, according to local custom," then "the priest gives the sign of peace to the deacon or minister." Nothing is said about offering it to others. According to the *General Instructions of the Roman Missal,* No. 112, "the priest may give the sign of peace to the ministers." The reason for this is that he has already given the sign of peace to all present when he addressed them in a global embrace with the words, "The peace of the Lord be with you always," to which all responded: "And also with you."

3

Celebration of Baptism

Baptism is the sacrament of spiritual regeneration by which a person becomes a member of Christ's Mystical Body, receives grace and is cleansed of original sin. The following are basic guidelines for the sacrament of baptism.

• To maintain and preserve the authentic symbolism of the sacrament of baptism, the water employed should be pure, true water. Nothing else is envisioned as valid matter. For reasons of health and sanitation, the water used ought to be clean. Frequently, if the water is left in the font it becomes stagnant. The minister should take steps to rigorously guard against this happening.

• The baptismal font itself ought to be attractive and in keeping with the architectural design of the church. Likewise this font should be clean and sanitary.

• There will be times, especially during the winter months, when provisions should be made to allow for the heating of the baptismal water.

• Except in the case of necessity, the priest or deacon should employ only water that has been specifically blessed for use in the rite. The Easter water (water blessed and consecrated at the Easter vigil to signify the relationship baptism holds to the paschal mystery of Christ) should be used during the Easter season. However, care is to be taken so that this water does not become stagnant, i.e., unsightly, odorous, or in any way offensive to those partaking in the celebration. Outside the Easter season, it is desirable that the water to be used in baptism be blessed at the time of the ceremony so that the words of blessing might exhort the faithful to recall the Lord's paschal mystery and clearly signify the salvation mystery which the Church is endeavoring to proclaim. In cases where the baptismal font is equipped with flowing water, the blessing is given to the water as it flows.

• The two rites of baptism — immersion or infusion — are valid and may lawfully be used in the sacred celebration of this sacrament.

• The words of baptism (form of the sacrament) in the Latin Church are: "I baptize you in the name of the Father, and of the Son, and of the Holy Spirit."

• Following upon the Easter season, the paschal candle (Easter candle) ought always to be given a place of honor in the baptistry, or wherever in the church baptism usually takes place. This is done so that the candle of the newly baptized might be lighted from it to show the relationship between Christ and the baptized.

• As with all sacramental celebrations, baptism is greatly enhanced by the use of hymns or songs — relevant to the sacrament. Songs of its nature stimulate unity among the faithful and it signifies the Easter joy which accompanies baptism.

• As with all the sacraments, the minister, mindful of the great liturgical renewal, should employ the various options allowed in the rite itself. The determining factor in one's choice of option must always be the particular circumstance and need of the faithful, as well as the family's particular wishes.

• The usual day for the celebration of baptism is Sunday. (Of course the preeminent time for baptizing is during the Easter vigil.) On Sunday, baptism may be celebrated during Mass. However, this can be impractical at times. The minister's good judgment should be employed when the celebration of baptism within Mass is requested. The celebration of baptism and Eucharist is exhorted. Some pastors designate a particular Sunday of the month and a particular Mass for the administration of baptism within the Eucharistic celebration.

• The priest or deacon who has performed a baptism should take care that the record of baptism be duly recorded in the proper book without delay. The substance of what might be recorded includes: (a) the name of the baptized; (b) the presiding minister, the parents and godparents, the date and place of the baptism (never presume that a secretary will properly record a baptism — this is not the secretary's responsibility); (c) a certificate of baptism should be issued to the baptized.

4

Sacrament of Reconciliation

On December 2, 1973, the Apostolic See promulgated a revised rite for the sacrament of penance or reconciliation. This rite became effective in 1977, and its use is mandated for the universal Church. Any practice to the contrary is no longer permitted.

However, to avoid confusion at the outset, we would like to make it clear that this rite in no way supplants nor eliminates the practice of private auricular confession. What the rite does provide is variety of celebration and the opportunity for adaptation to particular pastoral circumstances. This follows the thrust of renewal unleashed at the Second Vatican Council which sought to provide the Church with fluid, flexible and pastoral celebration of the sacraments.

The essential parts of the sacrament of reconciliation remain unchanged: contrition, confession of sins, act of penance (satisfaction), absolution. As long as these four elements are present, the sacrament of reconciliation is valid and fruitful. What this means, of course, is that while variety of celebration is offered in the revised rite and the more effective use of Sacred Scripture is exhorted, one ought not to conclude either that the sacrament has been changed or the use of private confession discouraged.

In the rite of penance, the competent minister of the sacrament is a priest having the required faculties, in accordance with Canon Law. However, it is to be remembered that all priests, no matter what their canonical standing, absolve validly all penitents in danger of death.

Good pastoral practice dictates that the clergy not rush headlong into incorporating the revised rite without properly catechizing the faithful, and never at the expense of downgrading or dismissing the "old" form for private confession. What the rite clearly shows is that penance room confession and communal penance services are but varietal forms of the sacrament of reconciliation, not the only form. The time-honored tradition of private confession ought always to be respected and honored. It represents a venerable tradition in the Church.

The sacrament of reconciliation may be celebrated in any place or location prescribed by law. Penance can be celebrated any time of day or night. As for the proper liturgical garb employed by the priest, the regulations set down by the local ordinary are to be observed. One should check with his local liturgical commission to ascertain what regulations are in effect in his diocese. In any event, one's discretion and good pastoral judgment in this matter is essential.

Besides the rite for reconciliation of individual penitents (private confession), the rite provides for the rite of reconciliation of several penitents with individual confession and absolution and for those cases when general absolution in the form of a rite may be given. As for the use of the rite of reconciliation of several penitents with individual confession and absolution, this is the basic communal penance service which has been actively employed by liturgists and parish priests for several years now. Since this form of the sacrament is handled in the following section, we defer our commentary until we come to discuss this form of the sacrament along with some actual penance services.

The form, character and regulation of general absolution is quite involved and should be treated carefully. Clearly, few will have need of this, for penance and the occasion in which this can be employed will forever remain quite rare. Nonetheless, it behooves us to speak to the issue of general absolution and offer our observations on this important form of sacramental penance.

The rite of penance incorporating the norms governing general absolution issued on June 16, 1972, by the Sacred Congregation for the Doctrine of the Faith, states that individual, integral confession and absolution remain the only ordinary manner of sacramental reconciliation, provided there exists no moral or physical impossibility in which case the individual is excused from the usual manner of confession. The revised rite is quite clear on the point that general absolution is not lawful when confessors are available in situations foreseen as being difficult (e.g., on major feasts and pilgrimages).

It is reserved to the bishops of the diocese to judge as to the presence or absence of the condition necessary for general absolution, namely, in view of the number of penitents, sufficient confessors are not available to hear individual confessions properly within a suitable time period, so that the penitents would, through no fault of their own, have to go without sacramental grace or Holy Communion for a long time.

The regulations continue to note that apart from the case determined by the bishops when general absolution may be given, if serious need arises for giving sacramental absolution to several persons, the priest must have recourse to the ordinary beforehand, when this is possible. One must remember that Canon Law understands recourse to mean by *mail,* but *only* for lawful celebration. Otherwise, the priest is to inform the local ordinary of the need and fact that he gave general absolution.

In order for the faithful to be validly absolved they themselves must be sorry for their sins, resolve not to sin again, resolve to confess in due time each one of the grave sins (within a year) and perform some sort of penance in satisfaction for their sins.

In short, general absolution is gravely restricted to avoid abuse of the sacrament. But when genuine pastoral need dictates the employment of general absolution it may be given, but the bishop must be informed. Basically, the serious pastoral need is a ministerial judgment on the part of the priest. This should not be engaged in lightly. In any event, unless a battlefield situation or some similar emergency or natural disaster exists, a short rite should be employed in the conferring of general absolution (perhaps a prayer, song, Confiteor, Our Father, and some sign of repentance, e.g., bowing of head, kneeling, etc.).

The revised rite provides flexibility for adaptation; it should be employed with discretion, keeping in mind that people change and grow very slowly.

Proper Dress for Penance Rites

The local ordinary can determine and regulate the use of liturgical vestments for the various forms of the sacrament of penance. Listed below are suggested regulations.

For Scheduled Celebrations of Penance: These apply not only to communal celebrations but also to individual reconciliation which is offered at regular and announced times, such as Saturday afternoon and evening.

Individual Reconciliation: This is the first form of the rite, without communal preparation, in the confessional or in a reconciliation room. The priest has a choice of being vested in one of the following ways: (a) in alb and stole; (b) in cassock, surplice and stole (the wearing of the cassock only, without the surplice, is prohibited); (c) black suit and stole (the wearing of a clerical shirt without a suit coat is prohibited).

Reconciliation of Several Penitents With Individual Confession and Absolution: This is the communal celebration in which the priest (or priests as the case may be) presides over communal preparation for the sacrament, usually from the sanctuary area. All ministers of the sacrament are to be vested in alb and stole. The wearing of a suit and stole is prohibited.

Outside Scheduled Celebrations: When a priest is spontaneously asked by a person to administer the sacrament of penance, he is not required to wear any specifically liturgical vestment. If a stole of good design and reasonable length is available, he is encouraged to wear that.

5

Communal Penance

General Outline

Priests wear cassock, surplice and violet stole.
- Entrance hymn and greeting.
- Opening prayer by the celebrant.
- Liturgy of the Word.
- Homily based on the Scripture texts. (A short film may be presented in conjunction with the selected Scripture texts and homily or as a substitution for the homily.)
- Personal examination of one's sinfulness. (A period of meditation should follow the examination of conscience.)
- Common recitation of the Confiteor, Act of Contrition or one of the penitential psalms.
- Private confession and absolution.
- Recitation of a common penance (e.g., a psalm, a decade of the rosary or any other appropriate penance).
- Sprinkling of the congregation with holy water as a sign of cleansing. (This asperges, if accompanied by the public recitation of Psalm 51, may replace Psalm 38.)
- The sign of peace.
- Closing prayer and/or recessional hymn.

Guidelines

- The presiding minister is afforded numerous options and should feel free to innovate as he sees fit or as need demands. However, he should take care not to omit any of the essential parts of this ceremony (Liturgy of the Word, private confession with absolution, and common penance).

This form of sacramental reconciliation should not be excessively celebrated (generally no more than one a month). The seasons of Advent and Lent, however, are especially appropriate for such celebrations as are the occasions of parish renewals, prayer groups, confirmation, special feasts and the like. If celebrated with a view toward a particular group (e.g., children), the necessary adaptations of text, homily and songs are to be made.

Advance notice as to the time and place of the communal penance service is most important. This notice could be carried by way of an announcement or through the parish bulletin or newsletter. Notification ought to be given to the people at least twice before its date of celebration.

1. An appropriate number of confessors should be available to facilitate the smooth ordering of this celebration so as to make confessions manageable and to avoid undue delay. One or two confessors not familiar with the parish should be invited.

2. The confessors should be advised not to engage in extensive spiritual direction, counsel or questioning since this is not envisioned by the rite of communal penance. Even though the service is not based upon or determined by speed of execution, but rather founds itself upon the public or communal nature of repentance and admonition or exhortation, nevertheless the celebrant must be conscious and sensitive to the time element and not unduly prolong this sacred ceremony.

3. Those persons attending should likewise be afforded the option of a prepared meditation or some similar spiritual exercise to perform while they await the completion of confessions. Also, appropriate hymns might be sung at this time.

• One option which might be employed is a communal penance coupled with a healing service. In the event this option is used, the communal penance service proceeds as usual but with a laying on of hands by those priests and deacons there present and an anointing on the forehead with blessed oil.

Suggested Optional Texts for Communal Penance

OLD TESTAMENT — Daniel 9:3-7; Joel 2:12-13; Isaiah 1; 40:1-11; 42:1-7; 43:1-14; 65:1-7; Hosea 4:1-8; Leviticus 4:13-21.

PSALM TEXTS (lamentation or supplication) — 3; 5; 6; 7; 13; 22; 26; 27:7-14; 28; 31; 35; 38; 39; 42; 43; 51 (The Miserere); 54; 55; 57; 59; 61; 63; 64; 69; 70; 71; 80; 88; 102:1-12; 102:24-29; 109; 120; 130; 140; 141; 142; 143.

PSALM TEXTS (thanksgiving) — 30; 32; 34; 40:2-12; 66:13-20; 67; 107; 116; 124; 129; 136; 138.

NEW TESTAMENT TEXTS — Matthew 5:1-16; 5:17-20; 7:1-5; 25:31-40; 26:36-42; Luke 7:36-50; 10:25-28; 15:1-2; 15:11-32; 23:32-43; 24:36-47; John 4; 8:1-11; 9:1-41; 11; 13:34-35; 1 John 2; Ephesians 2:1-9; 1 Corinthians 13:1-7; Galatians 5:1-11; Hebrews 4:14-16; James 4:1-7.

Psalm 51

R.   Have mercy on me, O God, in your goodness.

V.   Have mercy on me, O God, in your goodness,

46

in your great tenderness wipe away my faults;
wash me clean of my guilt,
purify me from my sin.

R.   Have mercy on me, O God, in your goodness.

V.   For I am well aware of my faults,
I have my sin constantly in mind,
having sinned against none other than you,
having done what you regard as wrong.

R.   Have mercy on me, O God, in your goodness.

V.   You are just when you pass sentence on me,
blameless when you give judgment.
You know I was born guilty,
a sinner from the moment of conception.

R.   Have mercy on me, O God, in your goodness.

V.   Yet, since you love sincerity of heart,
teach me the secrets of wisdom.
Purify me with hyssop until I am clean;
wash me until I am whiter than snow.

R.   Have mercy on me, O God, in your goodness.

V.   Instill some joy and gladness into me,
let the bones you have crushed rejoice again.
Hide your face from my sins,
wipe out all my guilt.

R.   Have mercy on me, O God, in your goodness.

V.   God, create a clean heart in me,
put into me a new and constant spirit,
do not banish me from your presence,
do not deprive me of your holy spirit.

R.   Have mercy on me, O God, in your goodness.

V.   Be my savior again, renew my joy,
keep my spirit steady and willing;
and I shall teach transgressors the way to you,
and to you the sinners will return.

R.   Have mercy on me, O God, in your goodness.

V.	Save me from death, God my savior, and my tongue will acclaim your righteousness; Lord, open my lips, and my mouth will speak out your praise.
R.	Have mercy on me, O God, in your goodness.
V.	Sacrifice gives you no pleasure, were I to offer holocaust, you would not have it. My sacrifice is this broken spirit, you will not scorn this crushed and broken heart.
R.	Have mercy on me, O God, in your goodness.
V.	Show your favor graciously to Zion, rebuild the walls of Jerusalem. Then there will be proper sacrifice to please you — holocaust and whole oblation — and young bulls to be offered on your altar.
R.	Have mercy on me, O God, in your goodness.

Service of Communal Penance 1

ENTRANCE HYMN

GREETING May the grace and peace of God, Father, Son and Holy Spirit, be with you all.

CELEBRANT'S INTRODUCTION Let us all be mindful that we are in the presence of God. [Pause for a brief moment.]

Brothers and sisters in Christ, we assemble in the presence of God seeking his mercy for our mistakes and failures, mindful as we are that the Lord God is the fountainhead of grace and peace. So let us proceed to his altar of reconciliation, confessing our sins, beseeching the almighty Father in the name of our Lord Jesus Christ.

Father, in our weakness we waver again and again. We find it so hard to avoid our favorite sins. Today, do something new: reform our hearts and fill us with rejoicing by giving us no desire other than to live in your love and to proclaim your praise. We beg this favor of you through our Lord Jesus Christ, your Son, who lives and reigns with you and the Holy Spirit, one God, for ever and ever. Amen.

LITURGY
OF THE WORD

See the Appendix at the end of this chapter for alternate scriptural texts.

A Reading From the Letter of Paul to the Ephesians (2:1-10)
You were dead, through the crimes and the sins in which you used to live when you were following the way of this world, obeying the ruler who governs the air, the spirit who is at work in the rebellious. We were among them too in the past, living sensual lives, ruled entirely by our own physical desires and our own ideas, so that by nature we were as much under God's anger as the rest of the world. But God loves us with so much love that he was generous with his mercy: when we were dead through our sins, he brought us to life with Christ — it is through grace that you have been saved — and raised us up with him and gave us a place with him in heaven in Christ Jesus.

This was to show for all ages to come. Through his goodness toward us in Christ Jesus, how infinitely rich he is in grace. Because it is by grace that you have been saved, through faith;

not by anything of your own, but by a gift from God; not by anything that you have done, so that nobody can claim the credit. We are God's work of art, created in Christ Jesus to live the good life as from the beginning he had meant us to live it.
This is the word of the Lord.

HOMILY
(or some other appropriate option)

CELEBRANT Let us pause for a moment and call to mind the times we have sinned against God and failed one another.

RESPONSE The Confiteor.

CELEBRANT Let us together pray the Confiteor:
I confess to almighty God, and to you, my brothers and sisters, that I have sinned through my own fault in my thoughts and in my words, in what I have done and in what I have failed to do; and I ask Blessed Mary, ever virgin, all the angels and saints, and you, my brothers and sisters, to pray for me to the Lord our God.

PRIVATE CONFESSION AND ABSOLUTION
Consult guidelines for the use of some possible options during this period. Also, see the end of this chapter for the meditative essay on forgiveness, entitled *Courage Is for Forgiveness,* which might be passed out to the people participating in the penance service for their reflection during the hearing of confessions.

COMMON PENANCE

CELEBRANT We have confessed our sins as individuals and as a believing community. Now let us recite together Psalm 65 as our common penance:

Praise is rightfully yours,
    God, in Zion.
Vows to you must be fulfilled,
    for you answer prayer.
All flesh must come to you
    with all its sins;
though our faults overpower us,
    you blot them out.
Happy the man you choose, whom you invite
    to live in your courts.
Fill us with the good things of your house,
    of your holy temple.
Your righteousness repays us with marvels,
    God our savior,
hope of all the ends of the earth
    and the distant islands. . . .
You visit the earth and water it,
    you load it with riches;
God's rivers brim with water
    to provide their grain. . . .
You crown the year with your bounty,
abundance flows wherever you pass;
the desert pastures overflow,
the hillsides are wrapped in joy,
the meadows are dressed in flocks,
the valleys are clothed in wheat, . . .

SIGN OF PEACE

CELEBRANT   When the Lord stood in the midst of his apostles assembled in the upper room after his resurrection, he greeted them with the words, "Peace be with you." Following the Lord's example,

51

let us now exchange with our brothers and sisters a sign of peace.

CLOSING PRAYER

CELEBRANT   O almighty and ever-living Father, you tell us to remember not the iniquities of the past but to rely on your healing mercy; we stand before you in humble thanksgiving for granting us new life in Christ Jesus. May we now live not as those who have no hope, but as confident sons, freed from our sins to become the living stones of your temple. We ask this through Christ our Lord. Amen.

BLESSING
AND DISMISSAL

CELEBRANT   The Lord be with you.

RESPONSE   And also with you.

CELEBRANT   May the blessing of almighty God, Father, Son and Holy Spirit, descend upon you and upon all those you love, wherever they may be — today, tomorrow and forevermore. Amen.

RECESSIONAL
HYMN

Service of Communal Penance 2

ENTRANCE   Let us all pray Psalm 38:
O Lord, in your anger punish me not,
in your wrath chastise me not; . . .
There is no health in my flesh because
of your indignation;

there is no wholeness in my bones
    because of my sin,
For my iniquities have overwhelmed
    me;
    they are like a heavy burden,
    beyond my strength. . . .
O Lord, all my desire is before you;
    from you my groaning is not hid.
My heart throbs; my strength forsakes
    me;
    the very light of my eyes has
    failed me.
My friends and my companions stand
    back because of my afflic-
    tion;
    my neighbors stand afar off.
Men lay snares for me seeking my
    life;
    they look to my misfortune, they
    speak of ruin,
    treachery they talk of all day.
But I am like a deaf man, hearing not,
    like a dumb man who opens not his
    mouth.
I am become like a man who neither
    hears
    nor has in his mouth a retort.
Because for you, O Lord, I wait;
    you, O Lord my God, will answer
    when I say,
"Let them not be glad on my account
    who, when my foot slips, glory
    over me."
For I am very near to falling,
    and my grief is with me always.
Indeed, I acknowledge my guilt;
    I grieve over my sin. . . .
Forsake me not, O Lord;
    my God, be not far from me!
Make haste to help me,

O Lord, my salvation!

CELEBRANT Peace be with all of you, now and for-ever.

RESPONSE Amen.

INTRODUCTORY
REMARKS

CELEBRANT My brothers and sisters in Christ: none of us here assembled need be re-minded that we have much to be sorry for — our failures and mistakes, cal-lousness and thoughtlessness, our sins against justice and charity. We are all sufficiently in touch with our own weaknesses and that is why we gather to partake in this holy and healing sac-rament of reconciliation. Motivated as we are by God's love, let us pause for a moment and recall our sins.

CELEBRANT May almighty God look kindly on us, forgive us our sins, and bring us to ev-erlasting life. Amen.

CELEBRANT Let us pray.
O almighty and merciful Father, you sent your only begotten Son, our Lord Jesus Christ, to set us free from the bondage of sin, even as you freed the Hebrews from the bondage of Pharaoh. Listen, we beg you, hear our feeble cry of sorrow and release the healing power of your Son upon your people, so that through the power of al-mighty love we might find peace and reconciliation. Father, we ask this

54

through our Lord Jesus Christ, your Son and our brother, who lives and reigns with you and the Holy Spirit, one God, for ever and ever. Amen.

A Reading From the Holy Gospel According to John (8:1-11)

Then each went off to his own house, while Jesus went out to the Mount of Olives. At daybreak he reappeared in the temple area; and when the people started coming to him, he sat down and began to teach them. The scribes and the Pharisees led a woman forward who had been caught in adultery. They made her stand there in front of everyone. "Teacher," they said to him, "this woman has been caught in the act of adultery. In the law, Moses ordered such women to be stoned. What do you have to say about the case?" (They were posing this question to trap him, so that they could have something to accuse him of.) Jesus bent down and started tracing on the ground with his finger. When they persisted in their questioning, he straightened up and said to them, "Let the man among you who has no sin be the first to cast a stone at her." A second time he bent down and wrote on the ground. Then the audience drifted away one by one, beginning with the elders. This left him alone with the woman, who continued to stand there before him. Jesus finally straightened up and said to her, "Woman, where did they all disappear to? Has no one condemned you?" "No one, sir," she answered. Jesus said, "Nor do I con-

55

demn you. You may go. But from now on, avoid this sin.''
This is the gospel of the Lord.

RESPONSE   **Praise be to you, Lord Jesus Christ.**

HOMILY
(or some other
appropriate option)

PERSONAL
EXAMINATION OF
ONE'S SINFULNESS

CELEBRANT   **Let us now reflect for a few moments calling to mind our offenses and failures, singling out those for which we are most sorry, and praying that the Lord will unburden our hearts by granting us his grace of reconciliation.**

PRIVATE
CONFESSION
AND ABSOLUTION   Consult guidelines for the use of some possible options during this period. Also, see the end of this chapter for the meditative essay on forgiveness, entitled *Courage Is for Forgiveness,* which might be passed out to the people participating in the penance service for their reflection during the hearing of confessions.

COMMON PENANCE

CELEBRANT   **As a reminder of God's cleansing grace, I will now sprinkle all of you with holy water, while we pray together Psalm 51:**
Have mercy on me, O God, in your
        goodness;
      in the greatness of your compassion wipe out my offense.
Thoroughly wash me from my guilt
      and of my sin cleanse me.

56

For I acknowledge my offense,
    and my sin is before me always:
"Against you only have I sinned,
    and done what is evil in your
    sight." . . .

Cleanse me of sin with hyssop, that I
    may be purified;
    wash me, and I shall be whiter
    than snow.
Let me hear the sounds of joy and
    gladness;
    the bones you have crushed shall
    rejoice.
Turn away your face from my sins,
    and blot out all my guilt.
A clean heart create for me, O God,
    and a steadfast spirit renew within
    me.

Cast me not out from your presence,
    and your holy spirit take not from
    me.
Give me back the joy of your salva-
    tion,
    and a willing spirit sustain in me.
I will teach transgressors your ways,
    and sinners shall return to you.
Free me from blood guilt, O God, my
    saving God;
    then my tongue shall revel in your
    justice.

O Lord, open my lips,
    and my mouth shall proclaim your
    praise.
For you are not pleased with sacri-
    fices;
    should I offer a holocaust, you
    would not accept it.
My sacrifice, O God, is a contrite
    spirit;

a heart contrite and humbled, O God, you will not spurn. . . .

SIGN OF PEACE

CELEBRANT The Lord Jesus Christ offered his apostles a sign of peace. Following the Master's example, let us exchange a sign of peace and reconciliation with our neighbor.

CLOSING PRAYER

CELEBRANT Let us bow our heads in prayer.
Father, you have freed us from the bonds of death and given us the hope of everlasting life. But even immortality would lose its luster, were it not with you. Grant, then, that we may rise from sin and selfishness, so that when we rise from death it will be to new and lasting life with you. We make this prayer through Christ our Lord.

RECESSIONAL HYMN

Marian Penance Service

INTRODUCTORY RITE Priest greets the assembled, giving a brief introduction to the purpose of why they have gathered for the celebration of the sacrament of reconciliation. He invites the people to pause for a few moments of silence and to examine their conscience to prepare themselves for the sacrament they are about to receive.

OPENING HYMN A suitable Marian hymn, such as "Immaculate Mary"; "Hail, Holy Queen, Enthroned Above"; "O Most Holy One"; "Our Lady's Song of Praise"; "Psalm 100"; "Queen of Heaven."

CALL TO WORSHIP

PRIEST   In the name of the Father, and of the Son, and of the Holy Spirit.

PEOPLE   Amen.

PRIEST   The Lord be with you.

PEOPLE   And also with you.

PRIEST   Hail Mary, full of grace, blessed are you among mankind.

PEOPLE   Your life proclaims the greatness of the Lord our God.

OPENING PRAYER

PRIEST   Almighty Father, through the obedience of your servant Mary, the Word became flesh. As you raised the sinless Virgin Mary to share in the splendors of your kingdom, may we, your humble children, be given your grace so that we may always live in your presence without sin.
We ask this through Christ our Lord.

PEOPLE   Amen.

FIRST READING   Possible suggestions: Sirach 24:1, 3-4, 8-12, 9-21; Isaiah 61:9-11; Proverbs 8:22-31.

RESPONSE   Psalm 113.

ANTIPHON   Truly you are the most blessed of women; the Lord is with you.

PEOPLE   Praise, you servants of the Lord,
        praise the name of the Lord.
Blessed be the name of the Lord
        both now and forever.
From the rising to the setting of the
        sun

is the name of the Lord to be
praised.
High above all nations is the Lord;
above the heavens is his glory.
Who is like the Lord, our God, who is
enthroned on high
and looks upon the heavens and the
earth below?
He raises up the lowly from the dust;
from the dunghill he lifts up the
poor
to seat them with princes,
with the princes of his own people.
He establishes in her home the barren
wife
as the joyful mother of children.

ANTIPHON   Truly you are most blessed of women;
the Lord is with you.

SECOND READING   Possible suggestions: Revelation 21:1-5;
Romans 5:12, 17-19; Romans 8:28-30; Gala-
tians 4:4-7. Secular readings include: *Lumen
Gentium,* Nos. 61-62; *Marialis Cultus,* Nos.
56-57; *Mary, Mother of the Redemption*
[see page 65 of this chapter].

RESPONSE   Psalm 122.

ANTIPHON   Behold the handmaid of the Lord; let it
be done unto me according to your
will.

PEOPLE   I rejoiced because they said to me,
"We will go up to the house of the
Lord."
And now we have set foot
within your gates, O Jerusalem —
Jerusalem, built as a city
with compact unity.
To it the tribes go up,

the tribes of the Lord,
according to the decree for Israel,
to give thanks to the name of the
Lord.
In it are set up judgment seats,
seats for the house of David.
Pray for the peace of Jerusalem!
May those who love you prosper!
May peace be within your walls,
prosperity in your buildings.
Because of my relatives and friends
I will say, "Peace be within you!"
Because of the house of the Lord, our
God,
I will pray for your good.

ANTIPHON   Behold the handmaid of the Lord; let it be done unto me according to your will.

GOSPEL READING   Possible suggestions: Luke 1:26-38; Luke 1:39-47; Luke 2:27-35; Luke 11:27-28; John 2:1-11.

HOMILY

RITE OF
RECONCILIATION

CONFESSION
OF SINS

PRIEST   Calling to mind our trespasses and sins we now ask the Lord for forgiveness by saying:

PEOPLE   I confess to almighty God, and to you, my brothers and sisters, that I have sinned through my own fault in my thoughts and in my words, in what I have done and in what I have failed to do; and I ask Blessed Mary, ever virgin, all the angels and saints, and you, my brothers and sisters, to pray for me to the Lord our God.

LITANY OF
RECONCILIATION

PRIEST God our Father, you chose the Virgin Mary to be your unique human instrument in the redemption of the world. We now pray that through her intercession, we may experience your mercy and forgiveness.

RESPONSE
(to be said after each petition) You who were free from sin, intercede for us.

PETITIONS • When we are tempted to seek our will instead of the will of the Father, we pray: *You who were free from sin, intercede for us.*

• When we intentionally close ourselves to the word of the Lord, we pray . . .

• When we fail to see the trials given us as our means to eternal life, we pray . . .

• When we fail to glorify the Lord for all the good things he has given us, we pray . . .

• When we only use the things of this world to satisfy our own selfish desires, we pray . . .

• When we allow ourselves to become a source of division instead of reconciliation, we pray . . .

• When we prefer words to deeds, and our needs above the needs of others, we pray . . .

- When we place more emphasis on man's law than the laws of God, we pray . . .

PRIEST God, the Father of all creation, grant that we may never be parted from your love.
Through the intercession of our Blessed Mother we ask that we may be granted a generous heart so as always to enjoy the fruits of redemption.
We ask this through Christ our Lord.

PEOPLE Amen.

INVITATION TO INDIVIDUAL CONFESSION After all those who desire individual confession have received the sacrament, the celebrant of the communal penance service will lead the people in the recitation of the canticle of Mary, from Chapter 1 of Luke.

ALL My soul proclaims the greatness of the Lord
and my spirit exults in God my savior;
because he has looked upon his lowly handmaid.
Yes, from this day forward all generations will call me blessed,
for the Almighty has done great things for me.
Holy is his name,
and his mercy reaches from age to age for those who fear him.
He has shown the power of his arm,
he has routed the proud of heart.
He has pulled down princes from their thrones and exalted the lowly.
The hungry he has filled with good things, the rich sent empty away.

He has come to the help of Israel his
   servant, mindful of his mercy
—according to the promise he made to
   our ancestors —
of his mercy to Abraham and to his de-
   scendants forever.

BLESSING
AND DISMISSAL

PRIEST The Lord be with you.

PEOPLE And also with you.

PRIEST Bow your head and pray for God's
blessing. [Pause.]

PRIEST Born of the Blessed Virgin Mary, the
Son of God redeemed mankind. May
he enrich you with his blessings.

PEOPLE Amen.

PRIEST You received the author of life through
Mary; may you always and every-
where rejoice in her protective love.

PEOPLE Amen.

PRIEST You have come with devotion to celebrate the mercy of God the Father;
may you return home with the joys of
the Spirit and the gifts of your eternal
home.

PEOPLE Amen.

PRIEST The Lord has freed you from your sins.
Go in peace and sin no more.

PEOPLE Thanks be to God.

CLOSING HYMN An appropriate Marian hymn.

Mary, Mother of the Redemption*

We tend to forget that the whole of Mary's early life was passed under the veil of a faith which neither saw nor comprehended, but continued to trust in the unfathomable dispensations of God's providence. We are prone to endow the Mary of history with a kind of intuitive vision of God in miniature, though this is never referred to either in Scripture or in tradition and is in fact contradicted in all genuine accounts, especially in St. Luke's Gospel. Often we fail completely to grasp her true greatness: Mary's life of faith.

Mary spent the whole of her life in the severe ordeal of this faith — not comprehending, but believing, with a faith which increased through meditation and through living in close contact with the growing Child. St. Luke says this in so many words — "But they did not understand what he meant" (Luke 2:50). This inspired text is of the greatest importance for us. In the Middle Ages it was popularly believed that Mary had a vision of the whole of Christ's life in all its phases at the moment of the Annunciation. This is, however, a false view, which deprives Mary of her greatness and of her great suffering, both of which are derived from the darkness of a faith which surrenders unconditionally to an uncomprehended mystery and an unknown future. Mary's life of faith on this earth is much closer to our own than the legends that have gathered around the Holy Family. If we realize this, Mary's example will have a very much more powerful impact upon our own lives — she experienced the same difficulties in life as we do in ours, but always she submitted, in faith and in prayerful meditation, to the incomprehensive events of her life of which God was the author.

Appendix of Scriptural Texts
for Communal Penance Service

ALTERNATE
SCRIPTURAL
TEXTS

A Reading From the Prophet Joel (2:12-13)

"But now, now — it is Yahweh who speaks —
come back to me with all your heart,
fasting, weeping, mourning."
Let your hearts be broken, not your garments torn,
turn to Yahweh your God again,
for he is all tenderness and compassion,

---

*Excerpted with permission from Edward Schillebeeckx's book of the same title.

slow to anger, rich in graciousness,
and ready to relent.
This is the word of the Lord.

A Reading From the Prophet Daniel (9:3-8)
I turned my face to the Lord God begging for time to pray and to plead with fasting, sackcloth and ashes. I pleaded with Yahweh my God and made this confession:
"O Lord, God great and to be feared, you keep the covenant and have kindness for those who love you and keep your commandments: we have sinned, we have done wrong, we have acted wickedly, we have betrayed your commandments and your ordinances and turned away from them. We have not listened to your servants the prophets, who spoke in your name to our kings, our princes, our ancestors, and to all the people of the land. Integrity, Lord, is yours; ours the look of shame we wear today, we, the people of Judah, the citizens of Jerusalem, the whole of Israel, near and far away, in every country to which you have dispersed us because of the treason we have committed against you."
This is the word of the Lord.

A Reading From the Prophet Isaiah (43:8-11)
Bring forward the people that . . .
        [are] blind, yet . . . [have]
        eyes,
that . . . [are] deaf and yet . . . [have]
        ears.
Let all the nations muster
and assemble with every race.

Which of them ever declared this
or foretold this in the past?
Let them bring their witnesses to
prove them right,
let men hear them so that they may
say, "It is true."
You yourselves are my witnesses — it
is Yahweh who speaks —
my servants whom I have chosen,
that men may know and believe me
and understand that it is I.
No god was formed before me,
nor will be after me.
I, I am Yahweh; there is no savior but
me.
This is the word of the Lord.

ALTERNATE
PSALM TEXTS

PSALM 107   If used antiphonally, use the following response.

R.   Give thanks to Yahweh, for he is good,
his love is everlasting.

V.   Some, driven frantic by their sins,
made miserable by their own guilt
and finding all food repugnant,
were nearly at death's door. . . .

R.   Give thanks to Yahweh, for he is good,
his love is everlasting.

V.   Let these thank Yahweh for his love,
for his marvels on behalf of men.
Let them offer thanksgiving sacrifices
and proclaim with shouts of joy what
he has done.

R.   Give thanks to Yahweh, for he is good,
his love is everlasting.

V.   Others, taking ship and going to sea,

67

were plying their business across the
    ocean;
they too saw what Yahweh could do,
what marvels on the deep!

R. Give thanks to Yahweh, for he is good,
    his love is everlasting.

V. He spoke and raised a gale,
lashing up towering waves.
Flung to the sky, then plunged to the
    depths,
they lost their nerve in the ordeal,
staggering and reeling like drunkards
with all their seamanship adrift.

R. Give thanks to Yahweh, for he is good,
    his love is everlasting.

V. Then they called to Yahweh in their
    trouble
and he rescued them from their suffer-
    ings,
reducing the storm to a whisper
until the waves grew quiet,
bringing them, glad at the calm,
safe to the port they were bound for.

R. Give thanks to Yahweh, for he is good,
    his love is everlasting.

PSALM 86 If used antiphonally, use the following response.

R. Listen to me, Yahweh, and answer
    me.

V. Listen to me, Yahweh, and answer
    me,
poor and needy as I am;
keep my soul: I am your devoted one,
save your servant who relies on you.

R. Listen to me, Yahweh, and answer
    me.

V. You are my God, take pity on me, Lord,
I invoke you all day long;
give your servant reason to rejoice,
for to you, Lord, I lift my soul.

R. Listen to me, Yahweh, and answer me.

V. Lord, you are good and forgiving,
most loving to all who invoke you;
Yahweh, hear my prayer,
listen to me as I plead.

R. Listen to me, Yahweh, and answer me.

V. Lord, in trouble I invoke you,
and you answer my prayer;
there is no god to compare with you,
no achievement to compare with yours.

R. Listen to me, Yahweh, and answer me.

ADDITIONAL SCRIPTURAL TEXTS

A Reading From the Holy Gospel According to Matthew (5:13-16)
"You are the salt of the earth. But if salt becomes tasteless, what can make it salty again? It is good for nothing, and can only be thrown out to be trampled underfoot by men.
"You are the light of the world. A city built on a hilltop cannot be hidden. No one lights a lamp to put it under a tub; they put it on the lampstand where it shines for everyone in the house. In the same way your light must shine in the sight of men, so that, seeing your good

works, they may give praise to your Father in heaven.''
This is the gospel of the Lord.

A Reading From the Holy Gospel According to Matthew (7:1-5)
"Do not judge, you will not be judged; because the judgments you give are the judgments you will get, and the amount you measure out is the amount you will be given. Why do you observe the splinter in your brother's eye and never notice the plank in your own? How dare you say to your brother, 'Let me take the splinter out of your eye,' when all the time there is a plank in your own? Hypocrite! Take the plank out of your own eye first, and then you will see clearly enough to take the splinter out of your brother's eye.''
This is the gospel of the Lord.

A Reading From the Book of Hebrews (4:14-16)
Since in Jesus, the Son of God, we have the supreme high priest who has gone through to the highest heaven, we must never let go of the faith that we have professed. For it is not as if we had a high priest who was incapable of feeling our weaknesses with us; but we have one who has been tempted in every way that we are, though he is without sin. Let us be confident, then, in approaching the throne of grace, that we shall have mercy from him and find grace when we are in need of help.
This is the word of the Lord.

Courage Is for Forgiveness*

Perhaps no virtue counts so highly in the Lord's book of life like that of true sorrow and mercy. God loves mercy because he himself is the author of mercy. He holds the man of mercy in the palm of his gentle hand; he desires to be close to this man for he sees himself in this person's reflection. Mercy is forgiveness, and a forgiving heart is a heart captured by the spirit. Peace reigns within that heart and so does the kingdom of God, for his kingdom is an empire of peace ruled by a heart of love.

Whenever I am asked to give a description of true manhood or enumerate the elements that go into making a saint, I always find myself coming up with one answer: the man who stands in readiness to forgive others, often those least deserving of it, the man who is not too ashamed to admit he has failed, nor too proud to ask for forgiveness. There is a certain *shalom,* or peace, to this man's life, a degree of wholeness, a measure of integrity. The man of forgiveness discovers he has many friends, for his heart is truly very attractive. This man is never lonely, even when alone, for the presence of others burns in his heart and his life has found a home within the love of another.

This forgiving man is a man of courage, for courage is not for conquering but for conciliating. Courage for Jesus was not leading a phalanx into battle, but doing battle with the forces that conjure up hatred within the human heart. Courage for the Lord was not for fighting but forgiving, not for ruining but repenting.

Jesus asked Peter not to draw his sword but to forgive what evil men were about to do that Thursday night. A repentant spirit is atomized through the gospels, permeating the depths, not only of those who are in a desperate way, but shoring up those of the kingdom who are trying with all their strength to love but are finding the demands more than they alone can bear. This spirit is the spirit of mercy given to the world as a scepter, granted in a special way to the sons of God. It's a spirit which not only builds up

---

*Essay on forgiveness to be used as a meditation during the hearing of confessions.

and enhances that love which is already present in the heart of man, but causes the very kindling of that loving spark.

The man of forgiveness is big enough to say, "I'm sorry," and gracious enough to accept another's apology. He allows others to humble themselves with grace. He knows how mercy is distributed for he himself receives it so often. One who recognizes his own failures can live with the faults of others. Sensing his own sinfulness he deals kindly with sinners. He makes more excuses for others than for himself. The benefit of the doubt comes very easy to him simply because he sees the good in others and overlooks the bad. Even the best of saintly lives are filled with regrets. A person who never becomes aware that he causes pain is a person who never knows what love is all about. One blind to the sorrow he inflicts is one who never hears himself utter a repentant word. A love that does not recognize its capacity for betrayal is not honest love.

To be called to Christianity is to answer the call to repentance. Throughout all biblical literature, only those who saw themselves as sinners in need of forgiveness were ever saved. Salvation history is filled with the stories of great men and their ability to apologize to God. David cries, "I have sinned against Yahweh." Isaiah laments, "I am a man of unclean lips." Peter cries, "I am a sinful man." The first step toward Jesus begins by admitting we have failed. By the same token a person who never turns to his merciful Father seeking forgiveness is an apostle (Judas) who is more concerned with a jar of ointment than a woman's (Mary Magdalene) first confession.

The world desperately needs forgiveness and only we can offer it to others. Love begins with forgiving, and hope is hollow without it. If the gospel is ever to have an impact on the modern world, its witnesses must exhibit this virtue. Forgive at all costs, for the kingdom of God is at hand.

6

Sacrament of Confirmation

I. Introduction

Liturgical Reform

Liturgical reform is an ongoing process in the Roman Catholic Church. Part of the Church's task is the restoration of liturgical rites according to an authentic biblical and ecclesial tradition. Through study and research we discover which elements of the current rites are the result of genuine growth and development in the Christian experience. This general restoration should enable the Christian community to understand and take an active and intelligent part in the new rites.

• The process of initiation into the Christian community involves the sacraments of baptism, Holy Eucharist and confirmation. These sacraments should be treated as parts of a continuing process.

• The rite of confirmation has been revised with the emphasis on the intimate connection which this sacrament has with the whole process of Christian initiation.

Dignity of Confirmation

In the sacrament of confirmation, baptized Christians receive the seal of the Holy Spirit, the gift of the Father. This gift of the Holy Spirit enables believers to become more closely identified with Christ for the building up of his Mystical Body in faith and love. They are so marked with the character or seal of the Lord that the sacrament of confirmation cannot be repeated.

Offices and Ministries in the Celebration of Confirmation

It is the responsibility of the whole parish community to prepare the baptized for the reception of the sacrament of confirmation.

• *Pastors* should see that all the baptized come to the fullness of

73

Christian initiation and are therefore carefully prepared for confirmation.

• *Parents* have a special responsibility to prepare their children for the reception of the sacrament of initiation. In confirmation they present their children to the pastor and bishop.

• *Catechists* help the parents and the pastor to increase in the children a knowledge of the faith. They also assist in the preparation for a fruitful reception of the sacraments.

• *The parish liturgy committee* (liturgists and musicians) have a special role to play in making the celebration of confirmation a genuine act of faith expressed in prayer and song.

The Ceremony

Attention should be given by all to the festive and solemn character of the liturgical ceremony, especially its significance for the local parish. It is appropriate for all the candidates to be assembled for a common celebration. The whole people of God, represented by the families and friends of the candidates and by members of the local community, should be invited to take part in the celebration and renew their own faith in the gifts of the Holy Spirit.

II. Liturgical Considerations

• There are two forms for the celebration of confirmation: (1) within the context of Mass; and (2) outside the celebration of Mass. We recommend strongly that confirmation be celebrated within the context of Mass. If for a good reason the pastor, having discussed the matter with the parish staff, decides that confirmation should be celebrated outside Mass, the bishop should be consulted.

• Careful planning and preparation involving the parish liturgy team, priests, sisters, catechists and parents, is important for a proper celebration of confirmation as it is for every liturgical celebration. From the beginning of the catechesis to the end of the ceremony, the theme of initiation should be clearly evident. All other themes such as the fullness of the Spirit, becoming a witness, accepting the role of prophet and participating in the ongoing Pentecost of the Church are secondary to the primary theme of initiation, although they are important considerations.

• Concelebration appropriately expresses the unity of the priesthood with the chief shepherd of the diocese and enhances the communal nature of the sacrament. Visiting priests therefore should be invited to concelebrate with the bishop.

• A special booklet containing the responses and hymns should be prepared for the ceremony. The scriptural readings and the prayers of the celebrant should *not* be included in the booklets.

• Music for both the congregation and the choir should be prepared well in advance. (Specific recommendations may be found in the "Music Appendix," at the end of this chapter.)

• Parents and friends should be notified well in advance that photographs may not be taken during the ceremony. This detracts from the sacredness of the occasion.

III. Catechists

It is understood that the initiation process into the Church is never a "fact" finalized at one specific moment in life. Confirmation is a most appropriate time to emphasize that belonging to Christ's Church is a matter of personal decision — a decision to become involved in the lifelong determination to be the Lord's "anointed one" (as pointed out in Luke 4:18-19) ". . . sent . . . to bring glad tidings to the poor, / to proclaim liberty to captives, / Recovery of sight to the blind / and release to prisoners, / To announce a year of favor from the Lord."

This decision of course must never be relegated to the sacrament of confirmation alone. All three sacraments of initiation are moments of ritualized decision. At baptism, the parents promise their personal involvement and support in the task. At confirmation, the individual candidate promises his personal involvement and support in the task. At confirmation, the individual candidate promises his personal involvement in the presence of the confirming bishop. In the Eucharist, the sacrament of commitment *par excellence,* the Christian constantly reaffirms his willingness to grow in the strength of that commitment.

Significance of Roles

• There is rich symbolism in the roles accepted within the total context of the initiation process: in baptism, the role of the priest and parents; in confirmation, the bishop and the individual candidate; in the Eucharist, the family and the parish.

• The parents or guardians present the candidate for the reception of the sacrament of confirmation. Having shared the faith with their children and guided their growth, they present them to the bishop for anointing and promise to continue to assist them in fulfilling their baptismal promises under the influence of the Holy Spirit. Therefore, by definition, the real sponsors for each confirmand are the parents or guardians. In extenuating circumstances, the baptismal godparents might be the appropriate second choice.

Significance of Material Signs

• The imposition of hands contains a wealth of scriptural meaning. It is important that time be taken to make its significance clear. This imposition is a calling down of the Holy Spirit by the bishop and priests (as shepherds and leaders standing in the place of Christ) upon the candidates. They pray that these candidates may receive the gift of the Spirit and the power to grow in wisdom and understanding of their responsibility to carry out Christ's mission as priest (to sanctify), prophet (to teach), and king (to lead). (Cf. prayer of the confirming bishop during the imposition of hands. Also John 10:10; John 15:13; Mark 1:22; Luke 19:1-4; John 7:46; John 10:14-15; John 5:12; Luke 7:18-22.)

• With the anointing of chrism, the bishop addresses each candidate with the approved rite. The concepts suggested in this action are: (a) the personal nature of the Gift (the Holy Spirit); (b) the origin of the Gift in the Father; (c) the relationship of sonship implied in the character of confirmation.

Methods Within the Classroom

• Steps must be taken to ensure that small groups are formed for instruction so that personal attention is given to each person being confirmed. Much of the potential beauty and impressiveness of the rite can be lost when the confirmands are treated almost on an assembly-line basis. The attention must ultimately center on the individual, not just the large group.

• There should be no distinction in the preparation of parochial school and CCD children. All are to have the same quality preparation. Moreover, there should be no distinction in the ceremony itself.

• Catechetical texts, filmstrips and other materials employed in the catechesis should highlight the initiation theme. Any catechetical tool which discusses confirmation alone, apart from the initiation process, is unsatisfactory. Materials are available through the local Office of Religious Education.

• (It is strongly recommended that a Bible penitential service be held on one evening before the celebration of confirmation. Candidates and parents should participate in this service. An opportunity should be given to parents wishing to make a private confession. Here is a golden opportunity to welcome back parents who have been away from the sacraments. Confessions of those to be confirmed should be heard before this service.)

• These guidelines should be read in their entirety by all those involved in preparing the candidates for confirmation.

IV. Notes for the Sacristan and Master of Ceremonies

• The bishop usually will bring his own alb. A cincture, stole and chasuble should be prepared for him. A chasuble of light material is preferred and of such length that the arms and hands have complete freedom of movement. The liturgical color is red or white.

• Concelebrants assisting the bishop on the right and left should be vested with chasubles. Other concelebrants may be vested in alb and stole although, if at all possible, chasubles should be worn by all the concelebrants.

• Other articles for the confirmation ceremony should be in readiness on the credence table: extra purificators, a quartered lemon, bread cut in quarters, an extra water cruet with hand towel, holy water and the Eucharistic prayer cards. Baskets of cotton are no longer necessary.

• Six Mass servers will be needed to assist in the following roles: crossbearer, two acolytes, paschal-candle bearer, crosier-bearer and miter-bearer. They should join the bishop and clergy at the beginning of the procession about ten minutes before the ceremony is scheduled to begin.

• Be certain that the public address system is functioning properly. It should be checked well in advance of the ceremony. The bishop may speak from the lectern. There may be need for a portable microphone.

• Should the class consist of more than one hundred candidates, Holy Communion will be given under the form of bread. If Communion is to be distributed under both kinds (by intinction), a sufficient number of chalices should be prepared on the credence table: one chalice for each Communion station, two for the concelebrants. Before Mass begins, two concelebrants should be assigned to each station during the distribution of Communion. The priest who distributes the host holds the ciborium while the assisting priest stands at his right with the chalice. All the chalices except the one used by the bishop should be prepared with wine before Mass begins.

V. The Commentator-Lector and Song Leader

• The commentator-lector and song leader can assist the worshiping community to participate more profitably in the liturgical celebration. They can also insure a uniform and smooth participation.

• The role of lector and commentator may be combined for this ceremony.

• The commentator should not detract from the celebration, calling undue attention to himself by excessive comments. The comments should be brief. If the ceremony is carefully carried out, it will need little explanation.

• The song leader should familiarize the congregation with the hymns and songs before the ceremony — briefly. A good selection of hymns, modern and traditional, makes for a better ceremony. It is not necessary to sing hymns constantly while the children are being confirmed; a few brief periods of silence or background organ music is recommended.

• Although many of the duties of the commentator will depend on the individual parish situation, the following suggestions will be helpful:

A. Before the ceremony begins, an introduction explaining the sacrament of confirmation should be presented. A brief explanation of the details of the ceremony will also be helpful. It will be useful therefore to familiarize the congregation with the booklet indicating the places of responses, the hymns, the procedure for the reception of Holy Communion, etc.

B. The Commentary

1. The Immediate Introduction

"Today we have gathered together to celebrate the sacrament of confirmation. In this sacrament, those who have been baptized continue along the path of Christian growth into the Church community, the path of initiation.

"This afternoon (this evening) the candidates for confirmation will receive the Holy Spirit, the same Spirit sent upon the apostles by the Father on the day of Pentecost. This gift of the Holy Spirit strengthens the Christian to bear witness to Jesus for the building up of his Mystical Body, the Church.

"The celebration of confirmation within the context of Mass emphasizes the fundamental connection of this sacrament with the Eucharist.

"Christian initiation into the Church reaches its culmination in the Communion of the body and blood of Christ. Our pastor and associate pastors as well as our guest priests concelebrate this Mass with our bishop to express the unity of the priesthood."

2. The Procession

"Let us stand and acknowledge the presence of Jesus and his Spirit in our community, in our bishop and our priests. The entrance hymn is [title] _____, number _____, page _____."

3. Liturgy of the Word

The first reading is read by the lector.

"Please be seated for the reading of the word of God.

"Our first reading is taken from the Old Testament, _____. In it the author states. . . ." (This should be a one-sentence summary, e.g., Isaiah 61:1-3: "The Lord anoints us and sends us to bring the Good News to the poor, to give them the oil of gladness. Listen to the word of God.")

The lector reads the scriptural passage.

The responsorial psalm is led by the lector.

The second reading follows the same procedure as the first.

The gospel acclamation is led by the song leader. If it is not sung, it is omitted.

The homily is then given.

4. Renewal of Baptismal Promises and Proclamation of Faith

"Confirmation is another step of initiation into the Church begun at baptism. Let us now stand. The candidates will renew the promises made in their name at baptism by their parents. After the renewal, the bishop will sprinkle all with holy water. We accept this reaffirmation of faith by singing the hymn, _____."

5. Administration of the Sacrament of Confirmation

The congregation will be seated during the anointing of the candidates. The candidates for confirmation should also be seated *before and after* the anointing.

6. General Intercessions

"We pray now for our own needs and the needs of the people of God all over the world."

The bishop will introduce the petitions by an invitation to pray. The lector will read the individual petitions. Members of the confirmation class may also be invited to offer petitions. The number of petitions should not exceed seven or eight. The bishop will say the concluding prayer.

VI. Order of the Rite of Confirmation

• The brief period just before the ceremony begins provides an excellent opportunity for an organ prelude. However, it should not delay the prompt commencement of the ceremony.

• The entrance procession is led by the crossbearer and paschal-candle bearer (side by side), followed by the lector carrying the Book of Gospels (high enough to be seen by the congregation). The lector is flanked by the acolytes. The non-concelebrating priests follow, then the master of ceremonies, concelebrating priests, the bishop and, finally, the miter- and crozier-bearers.

• As the procession enters the church, a joyful entrance hymn setting the theme of the celebration should be sung by both congregation and choir. It should have sufficient verses to last until the entire procession has reached the sanctuary.

• Greeting

The greeting should be in accordance with the usual rubrics.

• The Penitential Rite

The theme of the celebration may be incorporated into the penitential rite if Form "C" is used. (Form "C" may be found in any Sacramentary, specifically on page 475 of the OSV Sacramentary.)

• The Gloria

The Gloria is said on all days except during Advent and Lent.

• Opening Prayer

The opening prayer may be selected from the Sacramentary, e.g., the Mass of the Holy Spirit or the Mass of the day. On the Sundays of Advent and Lent, Easter, Solemnities, Ash Wednesday and the weekdays of Holy Week, the opening prayer is taken from the Mass of the day.

The opening prayer is read at the presidential chair by the bishop.

• Liturgy of the Word

FIRST READING

The Scripture readings for the celebration of confirmation offer many options. The readings may be selected, whole or in part, from the Mass of the day. They should be chosen in advance so that the bishop, lector and candidates for confirmation have time for an adequate reflection and preparation.

One of two lay readers should be invited to read the first reading. It is recommended that a woman be chosen for one of the readings.

RESPONSORIAL PSALM

The responsorial psalm is chosen as a reflection of our heritage in the Israelite community.

If the first reading is taken from the New Testament, the responsorial psalm is a meditation tying our Christian roots to the Old Testament.

SECOND READING

The gospel acclamation leading to the proclamation of the gospel should be sung. If it is not sung, it is omitted.

GOSPEL

• *Presentation of the Candidates to the Bishop*

The pastor and parents (or guardians) present the candidates to the bishop.

As the pastor approaches the lectern, all except the candidates should be invited to stand.

The candidates should be invited to stand at this point.

• *Homily*

The bishop delivers the homily.

• *Renewal of Baptismal Promises*

Since baptism is the first sacrament of the experience of Christian initiation, and since the parents presented the children for baptism, it is appropriate for all to accept the renewal of promises made by the candidates for confirmation. The acceptance of this reaffirmation by the congregation is signified by the singing of an appropriate hymn at the conclusion of the renewal of promises, during the baptismal procession. *(Only the candidates renew the promises.)*

• *Baptismal Procession*

The bishop proceeds down the center aisle sprinkling the congregation with holy water. A server carrying the paschal candle leads the procession. The bishop is also accompanied by the master of ceremonies and holy-water bearer.

A short baptismal song should be sung during this procession. As noted above, this song signifies the acceptance of the baptismal promises and is a reaffirmation of our own faith.

• *The Imposition of Hands*

The bishop stands at the altar flanked by the concelebrants and offers the invitation to pray.

All pray in silence for a short time.

The bishop and the assisting priests extend both hands over the candidates. The bishop alone says the prayer.

After the prayer, all are seated.

• *Anointing With Chrism*

The candidates for confirmation proceed to the bishop seated at the altar, or to the Communion rail. The bishop will ask each candidate his name. It is preferable to retain the baptismal name because of the emphasis on confirmation as a sacrament of initiation. However, the children have the option of selecting a special "confirmation name," provided it is that of a saint.

Proxies are not necessary since the parents themselves or the baptismal godparents present the children by their response to the bishop's question: "Why have you brought these children . . .?"

Foreheads are no longer wiped after the anointing.

Suitable hymns and songs should be sung by the congregation and choir during the anointing but not continuously. (Cf. "Music Appendix" at the end of this chapter.) The music should conclude as the last candidate is confirmed.

• Washing of Hands

Immediately after the anointing with chrism, the bishop will wash his hands using the lemon, bread and water. (Cf. "IV. Notes for the Sacristan and Master of Ceremonies," above.)

• The Creed

The Creed is omitted since a profession of faith is included in the renewal of baptismal promises.

• General Intercessions

These intercessions are models. If they are used, additional petitions should be prepared to include the sentiments of the community as well as the needs of the universal Church. This can be best accomplished by inviting the confirmands, parents and members of the parish liturgy team to prepare the petitions.

Articulate members of the confirmation class and representatives of the parish community might be asked to present individual petitions during the ceremony.

The number of petitions should not exceed seven or eight.

• Presentation of Gifts

The offertory procession should include a boy and girl from the confirmation class; one mother and father; and one Sister and lay teacher who have helped to prepare the children.

An appropriate offertory song may be sung. This is also a good time for an organ or instrumental solo.

• Prayer Over the Gifts

The prayer over the gifts may be selected from the Sacramentary, e.g., the Mass of the Holy Spirit or the Mass of the day.

• Preface

The preface of the Holy Spirit or the preface according to the season should be selected.

• *Holy, Holy, Holy*

Since the Holy, Holy, Holy is a hymn of praise, it should be sung. (Cf. "Music Appendix" at the end of this chapter.)

• *Eucharistic Prayer*

On Sundays it is customary to offer Eucharistic Prayer III; on weekdays Eucharistic Prayer II is offered.

• *Memorial Acclamation*

The memorial acclamation may be sung.

• *Our Father*

The Our Father may be sung.

• *Sign of Peace*

The gesture of peace attests to our belief that all things and all people will come together in unity in the next life. It also signifies our willingness to work now toward this unity. Here, the adults and children in the congregation should greet each other individually. No hymn should be sung during the exchanging of the sign of peace.

• *Lamb of God*

The Lamb of God may be sung as a litany during the breaking of the bread and the distribution of Holy Communion to the concelebrants.

• *Distribution of Communion*

The reception of the Eucharist under both species more fully manifests the sign of the Eucharistic meal as instituted by Christ. Since the sacrament of the Eucharist is a part of the initiation process, it is fitting to use the fullest manifestation of its symbolism. (Cf. "IV. Notes for the Sacristan and the Master of Ceremonies," above.)

• *The Reflective Period*

A brief reflective hymn may be sung during this period. If a hymn is not sung, there will be a short period of silent prayer.

• *Concluding Prayer*

• *Blessing*

• *Prayer Over the People*

• *Concluding Hymn and Recessional*

VII. The Rite of Confirmation Outside the Mass

- The order of the rite of confirmation outside the Mass follows the same order as the celebration of the rite within the context of Mass, including the general intercessions.
- The opening prayer and the Liturgy of the Word introduce the actual rite of confirmation.
- The ceremony concludes with the Our Father and the special blessing or prayer over the people.
- Benediction of the Blessed Sacrament is not celebrated.

Music Appendix

- *Criteria for Planning*

1. Message or theme of readings.
2. Personality of the worshiping community.
3. Evaluation of potential resources.
4. Aesthetic balance and beauty.

- *Preparation for Music in the Liturgy*

The music director should:
1. Know the themes for the day, season or occasion.
2. Familiarize himself with the readings.
3. Research for music that relates to the theme and spirit of the liturgy.
4. Consider the resources available in the parish:
   a. Type of choir.
   b. Congregational participation.
   c. Competence and experience of instrumentalists.
   d. Variety of Sunday liturgy.
   e. Cooperation with the chairman of liturgy and the liturgical coordinator.
5. Choice of music:
   a. The music should be chosen by the music director in consultation with the other musicians involved in planning the liturgy.
   b. The music and hymns must reflect the spirit of the liturgy.
   c. The amount of music used and the placement of music in the liturgy should be done fully and with the needs of the congregation in mind.
   d. The music should provide for:
      1) Flexibility and balance.
      2) Congregational participation.

3) An atmosphere of prayerful celebration inspired by the skillful use of the music.

• *Placement of Music in the Liturgy*

Depending on the music resources in the parish congregational participation, and type of liturgy, the following parts of the Mass may be sung:

1. Liturgy of the Word:
   a. Responsorial psalm.
   b. Gloria.
   c. Gospel acclamation (if not sung, omit).
2. Liturgy of the Eucharist:
   a. Holy, Holy, Holy.
   b. Memorial acclamation.
   c. Great Amen.
   d. Our Father.
   e. Doxology of the Our Father.
   f. Lamb of God.
3. Besides the above places:
   a. Entrance.
   b. Offertory.
   c. Communion.
   d. Meditation.
4. During the conferral of the sacrament.

• *Helpful Hints in Use of Music for Confirmation*

1. Before the ceremony:
   a. An organ prelude.
   b. An instrumental solo (flute, violin, recorder).
   c. Choral rendition (special arrangements for choirs).
2. Take time before the ceremony for a rehearsal (music to be used with the congregation).
3. Sensitivity to:
   a. Choice of the music and texts.
   b. Placement of hymns in the liturgy.
   c. The parts of the Mass that should be sung.
   d. Continuity of style and spirit.
   e. People in the congregation.
   f. Time element.
4. Need for a break between hymns at conferral:
   a. An instrumental solo.
   b. Short period of silence between hymns.
5. Keep sung parts of the Mass brief:
   a. Choose simple hymns, arrangements and familiar ones for the congregation.
6. The choir's function is to educate and enhance the liturgy. The choir should not be used to entertain or concertize.

7

Sacrament of Matrimony

(With Appropriate Homilies)

Marriage Ceremony With Mass

Preparations
• Usual vestments for celebrant and for concelebrants.
• Lectionary and Sacramentary.
• Holy water and incense.
• Tray for ring(s).
• Chalice, altar breads, wine, etc.

Marriage Ceremony Without Mass

Preparations
• Surplice, white stole and cope (if desired).
• Lectionary and Sacramentary.
• Holy water.
• Tray for ring(s).

Suggested Reading Before the Marriage Ceremony*

"I love because I love; I love in order to love."

Love is self-sufficient; it is pleasing to itself and on its own account. Love is its own payment, its own reward. Love needs no extrinsic cause or result. Love is the result of love, it is intrinsically valuable. I love because I love; I love in order to love. Love is a valuable thing only if it returns to its beginning, consults its origin and flows back to its source. It must always draw from that endless stream.

*Reading from the sermons of St. Bernard on the Song of Songs.

Love is the only one of the soul's emotions, senses and affections by which the creature in his inadequate fashion may respond to his Creator and pay him back in kind. When God loves, he wishes only to be loved in return; assuredly he loves for no other purpose than to be loved. He knows that those who love him are happy in their love.

The bridegroom's love, that bridegroom who is himself love, seeks only reciprocal love and loyalty. She who is loved may well love in return! How can the bride not love, the very bride of love? Why should Love itself not be loved?

The bride, duly renouncing all other affections, submits with all her being to love alone; she can respond to love by giving love in return. When she has poured forth her whole being in love, how does her effort compare with the unending flow from the very source of love? Love itself of course is more abundant than a lover, the Word than a created soul, the Bridegroom than the bride, the Creator than the creature. As well compare a thirsty man with the fountain which satisfies his thirst!

Can it be that all will perish and come to nought, the promised love of the bride, the longing of the creature here below, the passion of the lover, the confidence of the believer, simply because it is futile to race against a giant, or to contend with honey in sweetness, with the lamb in gentleness, with the lily in whiteness, with the sun in splendor, with Love in love? Not at all. Even though the creature loves less than the Creator, for that is his nature, nevertheless if he loves with all his being, he lacks nothing. One who so loves, therefore, has indeed become a bride; for she cannot so offer love and not be loved in return; in the agreement of the partners lies the wholeness and the perfection of marriage. Who can doubt that the Word's love for souls is prior to, and greater than, the souls' love for him?

Exhortation Before the
Sacrament of Matrimony

Dear friends in Christ:
As you know, you are about to enter into a union which

is most sacred and most serious, a union which was established by God himself. In this way he sanctified human love and enabled man and woman to help each other live as children of God, by sharing a common life under his fatherly care.

Because God himself is thus its author, marriage is of its very nature a holy institution, requiring of those who enter into it a complete and unreserved giving of self. This union then is most serious, because it will bind you together for life in a relationship so close and so intimate that it will profoundly influence your whole future. That future — with its hopes and its disappointments, its successes and its failures, its pleasures and its pains, its joys and its sorrows — is hidden from your eyes. You know well that these elements are mingled in every life and are to be expected in your own. And so, not knowing what is before you, you take each other for better or for worse, for richer or for poorer, in sickness and in health, until death.

These words, then, are most serious. It is a beautiful tribute to your undoubted faith in each other, that recognizing their full import, you are nevertheless so willing and so ready to pronounce them. And because these words involve such solemn obligations, it is most fitting that you rest the security of your wedded life on the great principle of self-sacrifice. And so today you begin your married life by the voluntary and complete surrender of your individual lives in the interest of that deeper and wider life which you two are to have in common. Henceforth you belong entirely to each other; you will be one in mind, one in heart, and one in affections. And whatever sacrifices you may hereafter be required to make to preserve this common life, always make them generously. There will be problems which might be difficult, but genuine love can make them easy, and perfect love can make them a joy. We are willing to give in proportion as we love. And when love is perfect, the sacrifice is complete. God so loved the world that he gave his only begotten Son, and the Son so loved us that he gave himself for our salvation. "Greater love than this no one has, that one lay down his life for his friends."

No greater blessing can come to your married life than

pure conjugal love, loyal and true to the end. May this love, then, with which you join your hands and hearts today, never fail, but grow deeper and stronger as the years go on. And if true love and the unselfish spirit of perfect sacrifice guide all your actions, you two can expect the greatest measure of earthly happiness that may be allotted on this earth. The rest is in the hands of God. Nor will God be wanting to your needs; he will pledge you the lifelong support of his graces in the holy sacrament which you are now going to receive.

Wedding Homily 1

It is most fitting and proper for a bridegroom and his bride to welcome and celebrate their wedding day with a unique sense of triumph. When all the difficulties, obstacles, hindrances, doubts and misgivings have been honestly faced and overcome, then both parties have indeed achieved the most important triumph in their lives. With the "Yes" that N. and N. will say to each other, they will have cheerfully and confidently defied all of the uncertainties and hesitations with which, as they know, a lifelong partnership between two people is faced; and by their own free will and responsible action they will have conquered a new land in which to live. Every wedding must be an occasion of joy — that human beings can do such great things, that they have been given such immense freedom and power to take the helm in their life's journey.

Certainly, you two have every reason to look back with special thankfulness on your lives up to now. Beautiful things and the joys of life have been showered on you and you have been surrounded both by love and by friendship. Your ways have, for the most part, been smoothed before you took them, and you have always been able to count on the support and love of your family and friends. Everyone has wished you well, and now it has been given to you two *to find each other* and to reach the goal of your dreams and desires. You know that no one can create and assume such a life from his own strength and that what is given to one is often withheld from another; and that is what is called God's guidance and providence. So today, however much you rejoice that you have reached your goal, you will be just as thankful that God's will and God's ways have brought you before this altar; and however confidently you accept responsibility for your action today, place it with equal confidence in the hands of God.

Many people today have truly forgotten what a home can mean. It is a kingdom of its own in the midst of the world, a stronghold amidst life's storms and stresses, a sacred refuge, a hallowed place, a sanctuary. It is not founded on the shifting sands of outward or public life, but it has its peace in God, for it is God who gives it, its special meaning and value, its own nature and privilege, its own destiny and dignity. It is a gift of God in the world, a place in which whatever may happen in the world — peace, quiet, joys, disappointments, heartaches, purity, discipline, respect, obedience, tradition, and with it all happiness may dwell.

And so today, you begin your married life by the voluntary and complete surrender of your individual lives in the interest of that deeper and wider life you two are to have in common. Henceforth you will belong to each other, one in mind, one in heart and one in affections. With this absolute trust and confidence in God, true love and a genuine spirit of sacrifice and devotion for each other, you can expect the greatest measure of happiness given to man on this earth. To love means to lose our autonomy and to become dependent on each other. All love is a gamble wherein we risk the best and deepest part of ourselves. There are no guarantees in this world to cover this gamble. We either accept love or we reject it. For this reason every act of love is more than an act of good will. It is an act of trust and an act of faith.

May, then, this genuine true love with which you join your hearts today, grow deeper and stronger as the years go on. This is the prayer and this is the wish of all your loved ones, here present, your relatives and friends, as they now witness your marriage vows.

Wedding Homily 2

Every wedding must be an occasion of supreme joy that two human beings can do such great things, that they have been given such an immense freedom and power to take the helm in their life's journey. A bridegroom and bride are perfectly aware that every day in their married life will not occasion all the happiness and good wishes and joy of their wedding day. When all the difficulties, obstacles, hindrances, doubts and misgivings have been honestly faced and overcome, then both parties have achieved the most important triumph in their lives. It is most fitting, I think, and proper for a bridegroom and his bride to welcome and celebrate their wedding day with a unique sense of triumph. With the "Yes" that N. and N. will soon say to each other, they will have cheerfully and confidently defied all of the uncertainties and hesitations with which, as they must know, a lifelong partnership between two people is faced; and by their own free will and responsible action they will have conquered a new land in which to live. But none of this can be accomplished without a true understanding of love.

In order to practice genuine Christian love two people, prepared to dedicate their lives to and for each other, must recognize that above all, love is a very personal relationship. God, the source of love, is a person. So man, made in the image of God, must also be a person. So must man be a person if he would not belie or betray his most fundamental reality, his created personhood. In trying to understand love, in order to practice it better, all of us, but especially married people, must continue constantly our reappraisal that love is the power to produce love. Erich Fromm insists that a person does not fall in love — he stands in it, he moves in it, grows in it, deepens in it. For if one loves without calling forth love, if he loves without creating love, if he loves without communicating love, he has demeaned and reduced the whole notion and beauty of love.

Genuine love is not counterfeit and cheap; it is disciplined, patient, kind, concerned and perseveringly courageous. True love refuses to hurt and willingly suffers for the object of its affections. Today we hear much of being a witness; it is the world of witness, the person sincerely involved in it is said to be a Living Witness.

And, certainly, you two have learned the genuine notion of love and are real witnesses of it to each other and to your many friends. You have every reason to look back with special thankfulness on your lives up to now. The beautiful things of life have been showered on you and you have been surrounded by both love and friendship. You have been able to count on the support and love of your families and friends. And now it will be given to you two to find each other and reach the goal of your dreams and desires. You know that no one can create and assume such a life from his own strength and that what is given to one is often withheld from another; and that is what we call God's guidance and providence. So today, however much you rejoice that you have reached your goal, you will be just as thankful that God's will and God's ways have brought you before this altar; and however confidently you accept responsibility for your action today, place it with equal confidence in the hands of God.

And so today, N. and N., you begin your married life by the voluntary and complete surrender of your individual lives in the interest of that deeper and wider life which you two are to have in common. Henceforth you will belong to each other — one in mind, one in heart and one in affections. With this absolute trust and confidence in God, true love and a genuine spirit of sacrifice and devotion for each other, you can expect the greatest amount of happiness and blessings given to man on this earth. May, then, this love with which you join your hearts today, grow deeper and stronger as the years go on. This is the prayer and this is the wish of all your loved ones, here present, your relatives and friends, as they now witness your marriage vows.

Wedding Homily 3

My dear friends:
You have just heard a description of holy matrimony

from the inspired word of God. Now you are about to enter upon this holy state. To impress you with the seriousness of this step, I should like to remind you that in the sacrament of matrimony it is not the priest but the bridegroom and the bride who are ministers of this sacrament. This is a wonderful thing. What does it mean?

As you have heard, sacraments are living encounters with Jesus Christ. In the sacraments, Christ enters into our lives now in order to give himself to us and so to help us accomplish a particular work for him. There is no more personal, nor more divine, activity in the world than one of Christ's sacraments. In most of the sacraments a priest is the instrument or the minister through whom our Lord acts as he enters into our life and our activity. But not in the sacrament of matrimony.

Here it is the two contracting parties who minister the sacrament to one another. This means that they bring Christ Jesus to one another. They do this when they give their mutual consent to the marriage contract, when they say "I do." So the "I do" or the "Yes" which each of you will pronounce, has tremendous implications. It means that you give Christ to one another; it means that you give yourselves to one another; it means that you give yourselves to Christ, that you give your consent to his working in you.

Up to now you have been more or less alone. Now you belong to one another and both of you to Christ. He invites you to live your future with him; and surely there can be no greater privilege. His invitation to you is what is called a vocation. He calls you to a life with him, a life of holiness, a life that leads to holiness. You are called to be saints in the particular vocation called matrimony, the vocation of the greatest number of people in the world. And Jesus calls you to holiness, not in spite of, but precisely because of your married life together, including the most intimate aspects of that life. Everything about marriage is holy and can lead to sanctity.

Your vocation in marriage consists essentially in living for the other party, daily, yearly, growing away from self and selfishness in order to find oneself in the beloved. Both of you must do this. If both of you learn to live for the other, your life will be a joy and your marriage a success. But if either of you continues to live for self, your marriage will be in danger.

You must have the deepest respect for one another as *persons*. You are not mere bodies, you are not some*thing*; you are some*one*, each of you. God's finest creation is the human person; and therefore we must have the highest reverence for all human beings; this reverence reaches its glory in marriage. Reverence, respect, kindness: this is the formula of happiness in marriage. Always be kind. Be kind and you will be saints.

Now you are about to enter upon this new life. And immediately after you give yourselves to one another, you are going to seal your marriage in the blood of Christ offered in this Mass. I repeat: in giving yourselves to one another you give yourselves to Christ. From now on your attendance at Mass will be different, more complete, more perfect than it has been before. Up to now you have given yourselves singly, by yourselves, more or less, as members of a parish community. That relationship continues, but now you make the gift together.

Then our Lord will come to you in Holy Communion. He will be the bond of your love for one another.

Now we are ready for the marriage. May I suggest that you enter upon this holy vocation with these words of the offertory of this Mass on your lips and in your hearts: "My trust is in you, O Lord; I say, 'You are my God.' In your hands is my destiny."

Wedding Homily 4

Symbols communicate more powerfully than words. This sacrament of matrimony is a sign and symbol; your rings are symbols, and actually the two of you are symbols, N. and N. "Symbol" is a fascinating word. It comes from two Greek words which simply mean "to put with" or "to put together." Originally, the word "symbol" stood for the insignia of a person's family identity. The insignia was divided into two or more pieces, given to the individual members of the family, and it was only when all the pieces of the insignia were "put together" that there was a symbol which had meaning and significance.

Your rings which you will exchange have meaning because there are two of them. N.'s [bride's] ring has meaning because it is a part of N.'s [groom's]. The rings symbolize that the two of you are joined in a loving relationship that has no end, just as the round rings have no beginning and no end. Even when you are apart, your rings remind you that you are still together. They are symbols of how you belong to each other — body, heart and soul. Once you take the symbols of the rings in matrimony, you can no longer live on your own, by yourself or for yourself. You must live for one another. For the symbol is not only on your fingers; you have sealed your hearts with love for each other. You are no longer two, but one flesh. You are no longer alone and single, but you are complete and you fulfill one another. This happens through the mutual love you vow before this gathering of friends and relatives.

But your rings are not the only symbols. Both of you together are symbols and reminders to all who love God. When we see you together, and witness your love and care for one another, you remind us of how God loves us. N. and N., you are symbols of Christ's love for us, his Church. Just as you choose one another in a lasting relationship of love in good times and in bad, so Christ chose us in love. Just as Christ will never stop loving us, so you cannot stop loving one another. When your rings are hot with anger instead of love, or cold with hurt or apathy after the heat of love has died down, your life together symbolizes the continued love you must have for each other. Why? Because your marriage is not only a sign of your mutual love, but it is also a reminder of Christ's undying love for all Christians.

This holy sacrament of matrimony which you freely and willingly enter today makes us all happy and want to celebrate. Jesus celebrated the wedding of his friends at Cana with a meal and he made sure there was plenty of wine for a good time. Our Lord is witness to your marriage today; he is happy to be present as you enter this contract, this covenant of tender and lasting love. Our covenant with

God is that he loves us and that we should love God by loving one another. N. and N., in loving each other you help each other keep your covenant with God. Love one another as Christ loved us: with joy and self-sacrifices; giving, giving, giving; body, mind, heart, soul and your whole selves. Then you become like Christ who loved us so much, he gave us his whole life, body and blood.

Become what you symbolize: you are no longer two but one; you can no longer take but you must give. Christ abundantly blesses your marriage for he knows what marriage is. Christ is married to his Church, his spotless bride. Nothing can separate Christ from his Church. Nothing can separate the marriage of the two of you which all of us come to witness and celebrate with Christ.

Celebration of a Wedding Anniversary

On the day of your wedding, you stood before the altar of God and solemnly vowed your love to each other. Today you stand before the altar, your family and friends, in striking testimony of what God's grace, conferred in matrimony can accomplish in a husband and wife who carefully guard and use the divine treasure that is in them. The world today has great need of the living sermon which your example of fidelity and love shows forth. You have been dauntless in the face of many problems and difficulties, known only to yourselves and hidden from others that could have made your marriage something entirely other than it has actually been.

We have every reason to believe that your married love has closely resembled Christ's love for his spotless bride, the Church, and that as Christ is the Savior of the Church, so you have been a savior to each other, helping each other grow in holiness and patience, but above all, true love for God and neighbor. And so, you have found in your life together true peace, dignity, happiness and security. The way has not always been easy. You have had to endure suffering together. But because you have been faithful to God, he has been faithful to you, blessed you abundantly and with his help you have been able to accomplish what you of yourselves without divine aid could never have accomplished.

You were married in Christ and Christ has continued these many years to be your portion in happiness and your chalice in sorrow. We beg him to guide you and watch over you, helping you to persevere in fidelity and love for the years ahead which we pray will be many and blessed.

Renewal of the Marriage Vows

HUSBAND   I, N., reaffirm my marriage vows and rededicate myself in the same spirit that I pronounced when I took you, N., for better, for worse, for richer, for poorer, in sickness and in health, until death.

WIFE   I, N., reaffirm my marriage vows and rededicate myself in the same spirit that I pronounced when I took you, N., for better, for worse, for richer, for poorer, in sickness and in health, until death.

PRIEST   Let us pray.
Lord, reach out your hand to your faithful servants, so that they may seek you wholeheartedly and receive from you all the good things they desire.
Almighty God, look with blessing on this couple who have just renewed their marriage vows. They have come before your altar with happy hearts to offer their thanks to you; grant that they may continue to live in genuine Christian love and attain with their family and friends the joys of many more years together. Amen.

Rite for Celebrating
Marriage During Mass

ENTRANCE RITE   At the appointed time, the priest, vested for
Mass, goes with the ministers to the door of
the church or, if more suitable, to the altar.
There he greets the bride and bridegroom in a
friendly manner, showing that the Church
shares their joy.

Where it is desirable that the rite of welcome
be omitted, the celebration of marriage begins
at once with the Mass.

If there is a procession to the altar, the ministers go first, followed by the priest, and then
the bride and bridegroom. According to local
custom, they may be escorted by at least their
parents and the two witnesses. Meanwhile, the
entrance song is sung.

LITURGY   The Liturgy of the Word is celebrated accord-
OF THE WORD   ing to the rubrics. There may be three readings, the first of them from the Old Tes-
tament.

After the gospel, the priest gives a homily
drawn from the sacred text. He speaks about
the mystery of Christian marriage, the dignity
of wedded love, the grace of the sacrament
and the responsibilities of married people,
keeping in mind the circumstances of this particular marriage.

RITE OF   All stand, including the bride and bridegroom,
MARRIAGE   and the priest addresses them in these or similar words:

PRIEST   My dear friends,* you have come together in this church so that the Lord
may seal and strengthen your love in
the presence of the Church's minister
and this community. Christ abundantly blesses this love. He has already

---

*At the discretion of the priest, other words which seem more suitable under the cir-
cumstances, such as *friends, dearly beloved, brethren,* may be used. This also applies to parallel instances in the liturgy.

consecrated you in baptism and now he enriches and strengthens you by a special sacrament so that you may assume the duties of marriage in mutual and lasting fidelity. And so, in the presence of the Church, I ask you to state your intentions.

The priest then questions them about their freedom of choice, faithfulness to each other, and the acceptance and upbringing of children.

PRIEST   N. and N., have you come here freely and without reservation to give yourselves to each other in marriage?
Will you love and honor each other as man and wife for the rest of your lives?

The following question may be omitted if, for example, the couple is advanced in years.

PRIEST   Will you accept children lovingly from God, and bring them up according to the law of Christ and his Church?

Each answers the questions separately.

CONSENT   The priest invites the couple to declare their consent.

PRIEST   Since it is your intention to enter into marriage, join your right hands, and declare your consent before God and his Church.

They join hands, then declare their consent.

BRIDEGROOM   I, N., take you, N., to be my wife. I promise to be true to you in good times and in bad, in sickness and in health. I

100

will love you and honor you all the days of my life.

BRIDE I, N., take you, N., to be my husband. I promise to be true to you in good times and in bad, in sickness and in health. I will love you and honor you all the days of my life.

If, however, it seems preferable for pastoral reasons, the priest may obtain consent from the couple through questions. First he asks the bridegroom:

PRIEST N., do you take N. to be your wife? Do you promise to be true to her in good times and bad, in sickness and in health, to love her and honor her all the days of your life?

BRIDEGROOM I do.

Then the priest asks the bride:

PRIEST N., do you take N. to be your husband? Do you promise to be true to him in good times and in bad, in sickness and in health, to love him and honor him all the days of your life?

BRIDE I do.

ALTERNATIVE FORMS In the dioceses of the United States, the following alternative form may be used:

BRIDEGROOM (BRIDE) I, N., take you, N., for my lawful wife (husband), to have and to hold, from this day forward, for better, for worse, for richer, for poorer, in sickness and in health, until death do us part.

If it seems preferable for pastoral reasons for the priest to obtain consent from the couple through questions, in the dioceses of the United States the following alternative form may be used:

PRIEST **N., do you take N. for your lawful wife (husband), to have and to hold, from this day forward, for better, for worse, for richer, for poorer, in sickness and in health, until death do you part?**

BRIDEGROOM **I do.**
(BRIDE)

If pastoral necessity demands it, the conference of bishops may decree that the priest should always obtain the consent of the couple through questions.
Receiving their consent, the priest says:

PRIEST **You have declared your consent before the Church. May the Lord in his goodness strengthen your consent and fill you both with his blessings. What God has joined, men must not divide.**

RESPONSE **Amen.**

BLESSING AND
EXCHANGE
OF RINGS

• FORM "A" •
PRIEST **May the Lord bless ✠ these rings which you give to each other as the sign of your love and fidelity.**

RESPONSE **Amen.**

Other forms of the blessing of rings are:

PRIEST　Lord, bless these rings which we ✠ bless in your name.
Grant that those who wear them
may always have a deep faith in each other.
May they do your will
and always live together
in peace, good will, and love.
(We ask this) through Christ our Lord.

RESPONSE　Amen.

PRIEST　Lord,
bless ✠ and consecrate N. and N.
in their love for each other.
May these rings be a symbol
of true faith in each other,
and always remind them of their love.
Through Christ our Lord.

RESPONSE　Amen.

The bridegroom places his wife's ring on her ring finger. He may say:

BRIDEGROOM　N., take this ring as a sign of my love and fidelity. In the name of the Father, and of the Son, and of the Holy Spirit.

The bride places her husband's ring on his ring finger. She may say:

BRIDE　N., take this ring as a sign of my love and fidelity. In the name of the Father, and of the Son, and of the Holy Spirit.

The general intercessions (prayer of the faithful) follow, using formulas approved by the conference of bishops. If the rubrics call for it, the profession of faith is said after the general intercessions.

General Intercessions
for the Marriage Ceremony

INTRODUCTORY
PRAYER Let us pray.
The Lord has promised that if we ask
the Father anything in his name, it
will be given to us. Therefore, with
confidence, let us pray.

RESPONSE
(to be said after
each petition) Lord, hear our prayer.

PETITIONS • Watch over, protect and guide your
holy Church, we beseech you hear us.
Lord, hear our prayer.

• Grant to all nations true peace and
understanding, we beseech you hear
us . . .

• Comfort the suffering, console the
lonely, protect the homeless, restore
peace to those troubled in mind or
body, we beseech you hear us . . .

• Make this marriage holy as you did at
Cana of Galilee, we beseech you hear
us . . .

• Grant through the union of your servants, N. and N., the grace of a new
Christian family, we beseech you
hear us . . .

• Give to this bride and bridegroom the
grace to bear witness to the holiness
of the married state, we beseech you
hear us . . .

• Renew by the Holy Spirit the grace of
this sacrament for all married people
here today, we beseech you hear
us . . .

CONCLUDING
PRAYER

Let us pray.
For those who love you, Lord, you have prepared good things that no eye has seen. Fill our hearts with fervent love for you; then, in seeing you in every creature and preferring you above every creature, we shall attain to those good things you have promised us, which surpass all desires. This love we ask for all here present, but in particular for our bride and bridegroom. We make our petition through Christ our Lord. Amen.

LITURGY OF
THE EUCHARIST

The order of the Mass is followed, with the following changes. During the offertory, the bride and bridegroom may bring the wine to the altar.
The proper preface is said.
When the Roman canon is used, the special Hanc Igitur* is said.

---

*HANC IGITUR

The words in parentheses may be omitted if desired, or as circumstances dictate.

PRIEST

Father, accept this offering
from your whole family
and from N. and N., for whom we now
          pray.
You have brought them to their wedding day:
grant them (the gift and joy of children and)
a long and happy life together.

(Through Christ our Lord. Amen.)

NUPTIAL
BLESSING

After the Lord's Prayer, the prayer, *Deliver us,* is omitted. The priest faces the bride and bridegroom and, with hands joined, says:

• FORM "A" •

PRIEST My dear friends, let us turn to the Lord
and pray
that he will bless with his grace this
woman [or N.]
now married in Christ to this man [or
N.],
and that (through the sacrament of the
body and blood of Christ)
he will unite in love the couple he has
joined in this holy bond.

All pray silently for a short while. Then the
priest extends his hands and continues:

PRIEST Father, by your power you have made
everything out of nothing.
In the beginning you created the universe
and made mankind in your own likeness.
You gave man the constant help of
woman
so that man and woman should no
longer be two, but one flesh,
and you teach us that what you have
united
may never be divided.
Father, you have made the union of
man and wife so holy a mystery
that it symbolizes the marriage of
Christ and his Church.
Father, by your plan man and woman
are united,
and married life has been established
as the one blessing that was not for-
feited by original sin
or washed away in the flood.

Look with love upon this woman, your
daughter,
now joined to her husband in marriage.
She asks your blessing.
Give her the grace of love and peace.
May she always follow the example of
the holy women
whose praises are sung in the Scriptures.

May her husband put his trust in her
and recognize that she is his equal
and the heir with him to the life of
grace.
May he always honor her and love her
as Christ loves his bride, the Church.

Father, keep them always true to your
commandments.
Keep them faithful in marriage
and let them be living examples of
Christian life.

Give them the strength which comes
from the gospel
so that they may be witnesses of
Christ to others.
(Bless them with children
and help them to be good parents.
May they live to see their children's
children.)
And, after a happy old age,
grant them fullness of life with the
saints
in the kingdom of heaven.

(We ask this) through Christ our Lord.

RESPONSE Amen.

If one or both of the parties will not be receiving Communion, the words in the introduction
to the nuptial blessing [above], *through the*

sacrament of the body and blood of Christ, may be omitted.

If desired, in the prayer [above], *Father, by your power,* two of the first three paragraphs may be omitted, keeping only the paragraph which corresponds to the reading of the Mass. In the last paragraph of this prayer, the words in parentheses may be omitted whenever circumstances suggest it; for example, if the couple is advanced in years.

Other forms of the nuptial blessing are:

• FORM "B" • In the following prayer, either the paragraph, *Holy Father, you created mankind,* or the paragraph, *Father, to reveal the plan of your love,* may be omitted, keeping only the paragraph which corresponds to the reading of the Mass.

PRIEST Let us pray to the Lord for N. and N.
who come to God's altar at the beginning of their married life
so that they may always be united in love for each other
(as now they share in the body and blood of Christ).

All pray silently for a short while. Then the priest extends his hands and continues:

PRIEST Holy Father, you created mankind in your own image
and made man and woman to be joined as husband and wife
in union of body and heart
and so fulfill their mission in this world.

Father, to reveal the plan of your love,
you made the union of husband and wife
an image of the covenant between you and your people.

108

In the fulfillment of this sacrament,
the marriage of Christian man and
woman
is a sign of the marriage between
Christ and the Church.
Father, stretch out your hand, and
bless N. and N.

Lord, grant that as they begin to live
this sacrament
they may share with each other the
gifts of your love
and become one in heart and mind
as witnesses to your presence in their
marriage.
Help them to create a home together
(and give them children to be formed
by the gospel
and to have a place in your family).

Give your blessings to N., your daughter,
so that she may be a good wife (and
mother),
caring for the home,
faithful in love for her husband,
generous and kind.
Give your blessings to N., your son,
so that he may be a faithful husband
(and a good father).

Father, grant that as they come together to your table on earth,
so they may one day have the joy of
sharing your feast in heaven.
(We ask this) through Christ our Lord.

RESPONSE Amen.

• FORM "C" •
PRIEST My dear friends, let us ask God

109

for his continued blessings upon this bridegroom and his bride [or N. and N.].

All pray silently for a short while. Then the priest extends his hands and continues:

PRIEST Holy Father, creator of the universe,
maker of man and woman in your own likeness,
source of blessing for married life,
we humbly pray to you for this woman
who today is united with her husband in this sacrament of marriage.

May your fullest blessing come upon her and her husband
so that they may together rejoice in your gift of married love
(and enrich your Church with their children).

Lord, may they both praise you when they are happy
and turn to you in their sorrows.

May they be glad that you help them in their work
and know that you are with them in their need.

May they pray to you in the community of the Church,
and be your witnesses in the world.

May they reach old age in the company of their friends,
and come at last to the kingdom of heaven.

(We ask this) through Christ our Lord.

RESPONSE Amen.

At the words, *Let us offer each other the*

110

sign of peace, the married couple and all present show their peace and love for one another in an appropriate way.

The married couple may receive Communion under both kinds.

BLESSING AT THE END OF MASS

Before blessing the people at the end of Mass, the priest blesses the bride and bridegroom, using one of the forms below:

• FORM "A" •

PRIEST

God the eternal Father keep you in love with each other,
so that the peace of Christ may stay with you
and be always in your home.

RESPONSE   Amen.

PRIEST

May (your children bless you),
your friends console you
and all men live in peace with you.

RESPONSE   Amen.

PRIEST

May you always bear witness to the love of God in this world
so that the afflicted and the needy
will find in you generous friends,
and welcome you into the joys of heaven.

RESPONSE   Amen.

PRIEST

And may almighty God bless you all,
the Father, and the Son, ✠ and the Holy Spirit.

RESPONSE   Amen.

• FORM "B" •

PRIEST

May God, the almighty Father,
give you his joy

and bless you (in your children).

RESPONSE Amen.

PRIEST May the only Son of God have mercy
on you
and help you in good times and in bad.

RESPONSE Amen.

PRIEST May the Holy Spirit of God
always fill your hearts with his love.

RESPONSE Amen.

PRIEST And may almighty God bless you all,
the Father, and the Son, ✠ and the
Holy Spirit.

RESPONSE Amen.

• FORM "C" •
PRIEST May the Lord Jesus, who was a guest
at the wedding in Cana,
bless you and your families and
friends.

RESPONSE Amen.

PRIEST May Jesus, who loved his Church to
the end,
always fill your hearts with his love.

RESPONSE Amen.

PRIEST May he grant that, as you believe in
his resurrection,
so you may wait for him in joy and
hope.

RESPONSE Amen.

112

PRIEST And may almighty God bless you all, the Father, and the Son, ✝ and the Holy Spirit.

RESPONSE Amen.

(In the dioceses of the United States another form may be used.)
If two or more marriages are celebrated at the same time, the questioning before the consent, the consent itself, and the acceptance of consent shall always be done individually for each couple; the rest, including the nuptial blessing, is said once for all, using the plural form.

Suggested Prayer of Bride and Bridegroom After Holy Communion

BRIDE AND BRIDEGROOM O God, our Father in heaven, we now kneel before you very happy, but somewhat nervous. We feel you brought us together in the beginning, helped our love grow and at this moment are with us in a special way. We ask that you stay by our side in the days ahead. Protect us from anything which might harm this marriage; give us courage when burdens come our way; teach us to forgive one another when we fail.

BRIDEGROOM I ask from you the assistance I need to be a good husband and father. Never let me take my wife for granted or forget she needs to be loved. If you bless us with children, I promise to love them, to care for them, to give them the best possible example.

113

BRIDE	I ask from you the assistance I need to be a good wife and mother. May I never forget how important my husband's work is for my happiness, or fail to give him encouragement. If you bless me with motherhood, I promise to give myself totally to the children, even to the point of stepping aside when they must walk alone.
BRIDE AND BRIDEGROOM	We ask, finally, that in our old age we may love one another and cherish each other as deeply and as much as we do at this very moment. May you grant these wishes we offer through your Son Jesus Christ, our Lord and Savior. Amen.

Rite for Celebrating
Marriage Outside Mass*

ENTRANCE RITE AND LITURGY OF THE WORD	At the appointed time, the priest, wearing surplice and white stole (or a white cope, if desired), proceeds with the ministers to the door of the church or, if more suitable, to the altar. There he greets the bride and bridegroom in a friendly manner, showing that the Church shares their joy. Where it is desirable that the rite of welcome be omitted, the celebration of matrimony begins at once with the Liturgy of the Word. If there is a procession to the altar, the ministers go first, followed by the priest, and then the bride and bridegroom. According to local

---

*According to the words of the *Constitution on the Sacred Liturgy,* the celebration of marriage normally takes place during Mass. Nevertheless, a good reason can excuse from the celebration of Mass (Sacred Congregation of Rites, Instruction, *Inter Oecumenici,* No. 70: AAS 56 [1964] 893), and sometimes even urges that Mass should be omitted. In this case the rite for celebrating marriage outside Mass should be used.

custom, they may be escorted by at least their parents and the two witnesses. Meanwhile, the entrance song is sung.

Then the people are greeted, and the prayer is offered, unless a brief pastoral exhortation seems more desirable.

The Liturgy of the Word takes place in the usual manner. There may be three readings, the first of them from the Old Testament.

After the gospel, the priest gives a homily (cf. Homilies, pages 90-97) drawn from the sacred text. He speaks about the mystery of Christian marriage, the dignity of wedded love, the grace of the sacrament, and the responsibilities of married people, keeping in mind the circumstances of this particular marriage.

RITE OF MARRIAGE All stand, including the bride and the bridegroom, and the priest addresses them in these or similar words:

PRIEST My dear friends, you have come together in this church so that the Lord may seal and strengthen your love in the presence of the Church's minister and this community. Christ abundantly blesses this love. He has already consecrated you in baptism and now he enriches and strengthens you by a special sacrament so that you may assume the duties of marriage in mutual and lasting fidelity. And so, in the presence of the Church, I ask you to state your intentions.

The priest then questions them about their freedom of choice, faithfulness to each other, and the acceptance and upbringing of children.

PRIEST N. and N., have you come here freely and without reservation to give yourselves to each other in marriage?

Will you love and honor each other as man and wife for the rest of your lives?

The following question may be omitted if, for example, the couple is advanced in years.

PRIEST Will you accept children lovingly from God, and bring them up according to the law of Christ and his Church?

Each answers the questions separately.

CONSENT The priest invites them to declare their consent.

PRIEST Since it is your intention to enter into marriage, join your right hands, and declare your consent before God and his Church.

They join hands, then declare their consent.

BRIDEGROOM I, N., take you, N., to be my wife. I promise to be true to you in good times and in bad, in sickness and in health. I will love you and honor you all the days of my life.

BRIDE I, N., take you, N., to be my husband. I promise to be true to you in good times and in bad, in sickness and in health. I will love you and honor you all the days of my life.

If, however, it seems preferable for pastoral reasons, the priest may obtain consent from the couple through questions. First he asks the bridegroom:

PRIEST N., do you take N. to be your wife? Do

116

you promise to be true to her in good times and in bad, in sickness and in health, to love her and honor her all the days of your life?

BRIDEGROOM   I do.

Then the priest asks the bride:

PRIEST   N., do you take N. to be your husband? Do you promise to be true to him in good times and in bad, in sickness and in health, to love him and honor him all the days of your life?

BRIDE   I do.

In the dioceses of the United States, the following alternative form may be used:

BRIDEGROOM (BRIDE)   I, N., take you, N., for my lawful wife (husband), to have and to hold, from this day forward, for better, for worse, for richer, for poorer, in sickness and in health, until death do us part.

If it seems preferable for pastoral reasons for the priest to obtain consent from the couple through questions, in the dioceses of the United States the following alternative form may be used:

PRIEST   N., do you take N. for your lawful wife (husband), to have and to hold, from this day forward, for better, for worse, for richer, for poorer, in sickness and in health, until death do you part?

BRIDEGROOM (BRIDE)   I do.

If pastoral necessity demands it, the conference of bishops may decree that the priest should always obtain the consent of the couple through questions.

Receiving their consent, the priest says:

PRIEST **You have declared your consent before the Church. May the Lord in his goodness strengthen your consent and fill you both with his blessings.**
What God has joined, men must not divide.

RESPONSE **Amen.**

BLESSING AND
EXCHANGE
OF RINGS

PRIEST **May the Lord bless ✠ these rings**
which you give to each other
as the sign of your love and fidelity.

RESPONSE **Amen.**

The bridegroom places his wife's ring on her ring finger. He may say:

BRIDEGROOM **N., take this ring as a sign of my love and fidelity. In the name of the Father, and of the Son, and of the Holy Spirit.**

The bride places her husband's ring on his ring finger. She may say:

BRIDE **N., take this ring as a sign of my love and fidelity. In the name of the Father, and of the Son, and of the Holy Spirit.**

GENERAL
INTERCESSIONS
AND NUPTIAL
BLESSINGS

The general intercessions (prayer of the faithful) and the blessing of the couple take place in this order:

• First the priest uses the invitatory of the blessing of the couple, or any other, taken

118

from the approved formulas for the general intercessions (cf. page 104).

• Immediately after the invitatory, there can be either a brief silence, or a series of petitions from the prayer of the faithful with responses by the people. All the petitions should be in harmony with the blessing which follows, but should not duplicate it.

• Then, omitting the prayer that concludes the prayer of the faithful, the priest extends his hands and blesses the bride and the bridegroom. This blessing, for example, may be, *Father, by your power.*

CONCLUSION OF THE CELEBRATION

The entire rite can be concluded with the Lord's Prayer and the blessing, *May almighty God.*

If two or more marriages are celebrated at the same time, the questioning before the consent, the consent itself, and the acceptance of consent shall always be done individually for each couple; the rest, including the nuptial blessing, is said once for all, using the plural form.

The rite described above should be used by a deacon who, when a priest cannot be present, has been delegated by the bishop or pastor to assist at the celebration of marriage, and to give the Church's blessing.

If Mass cannot be celebrated and Holy Communion is to be distributed during the rite, the Lord's Prayer is said first. After Communion, a reverent silence may be observed for a while, or a psalm or song of praise may be sung or recited. Then comes the prayer, *Lord, we who have shared* (if only the bride and bridegroom receive), or the prayer, *God, who in this wondrous sacrament,* or other suitable prayer.

The rite ends with a blessing, for example, *May almighty God bless you.*

Mixed Marriage Guidelines

Pope Paul VI issued in 1970 an "Apostolic Letter Issued Motu Proprio [M.P.] Determining Norms for Mixed Marriages." In that decree he left many decisions to the hierarchy of each country; our own National Conference of Catholic Bishops (NCCB) applied the Pope's guidelines to the United States in a document, cited below, which took effect on January 1, 1971.

Specific Norms

This apostolic letter on mixed marriages leaves to episcopal conferences the further determination of specific questions. (The norms of *Matrimonia Mixta* are not repeated here, nor are the special norms affecting the marriages of Eastern Catholics and marriages of Catholics with Eastern non-Catholic Christians. They are found in the *Decree on Catholic-Orthodox Marriages,* of February 22, 1967.) In order to implement this mandate, the NCCB sets forth the following for the dioceses of the United States.

• *Pastoral Responsibility*

1. In every diocese, there shall be appropriate informational programs to explain both the reasons for restrictions upon mixed marriages and the positive spiritual values to be sought in such marriages when permitted. This is particularly important if the non-Catholic is a Christian believer and the unity of married and family life is ultimately based upon the baptism of both wife and husband. If possible, all such programs should be undertaken after consultation with and in conjunction with non-Catholic authorities.

2. In every diocese there shall be appropriate programs for the instruction and orientation of the clergy, as well as of candidates for the ministry, so that they may understand fully the reasons for the successive changes in the discipline of mixed marriage and may willingly undertake their personal responsibilities to each individual couple and family in the exercise of their pastoral ministry.

3. In addition to the customary marriage preparation programs, it is the serious duty of each one in the pastoral ministry, according to his own responsibility, office or assignment, to undertake: (a) the spiritual and catechetical preparation, especially in regard to the "ends and essential properties of marriage [which] are not to be excluded by either party" (cf. *Matrimonia Mixta,* No. 6), on a direct and individual basis, of couples who seek to enter a mixed marriage; (b) continued concern and assistance to the wife and husband in mixed marriages and to their children, so that married and family life may be supported in unity, respect for conscience and common spiritual benefit.

4. In the assistance which he gives in preparation for marriage between a Catholic and a non-Catholic, and his continued efforts to help all married couples and families, the priest should endeavor to be in contact and to cooperate with the minister or religious counselor of the non-Catholic.

• *Declaration and Promise (M.P., No. 7)*

5. The declaration and promise by the Catholic, necessary for dispensation from the impediment to a mixed marriage (either mixed religion or disparity of worship), shall be made, in the following words or their substantial equivalent:

"I reaffirm my faith in Jesus Christ and, with God's help, intend to continue living that faith in the Catholic Church.

"I promise to do all in my power to share the faith I have received with our children by having them baptized and reared as Catholics."

6. The declaration and promise are made in the presence of a priest or deacon either orally or in writing as the Catholic prefers.

7. The form of the declaration and promise is not altered in the case of the marriage of a Catholic with another baptized Christian, but the priest should draw the attention of the Catholic to the communion of spiritual benefits in such a Christian marriage. The promise and declaration should be made in the light of the "certain, though imperfect, communion" of the non-Catholic with the Catholic Church because of his belief in Christ and baptism (cf. *Decree on Ecumenism,* No. 3).

8. At an opportune time before marriage, and preferably as part of the usual premarital instructions, the non-Catholic must be informed of the promises and of the responsibility of the Catholic. No precise manner or occasion of informing the non-Catholic is prescribed. It may be done by the priest, deacon or the Catholic party. No formal statement of the non-Catholic is required. But the mutual understanding of this question beforehand should prevent possible disharmony that might otherwise arise during married life.

9. The priest who submits the request for dispensation from the impediment to a mixed marriage shall certify that the declaration and promise have been made by the Catholic and that the non-Catholic has been informed of this requirement. This is done in the following or similar words:

"The required promise and declaration have been made by the Catholic in my presence. The non-Catholic has been informed of this requirement so that it is certain that he (she) is aware of the promise and obligation on the part of the Catholic."

The promise of the Catholic must be sincerely made, and is to be presumed to be sincerely made. If, however, the priest has reason to doubt the sincerity of the promise made by the Catholic, he may not recommend the request for the dispensation and should submit the matter to the local ordinary.

• *Form of Marriage (M.P., No. 9)*

10. Where there are serious difficulties in observing the Catholic canonical form in a mixed marriage, the local ordinary of the Catholic party or of the place where the marriage is to occur may dispense the Catholic from the observance of the form for a just pastoral cause. An

exhaustive list is impossible, but the following are the types of reasons: to achieve family harmony or to avoid family alienation, to obtain parental agreement to the marriage, to recognize the significant claims of relationship or special friendship with a non-Catholic minister, to permit the marriage in a church that has particular importance to the non-Catholic. If the ordinary of the Catholic party grants a dispensation for a marriage which is to take place in another diocese, the ordinary of that diocese should be informed beforehand.

11. Ordinarily this dispensation from the canonical form is granted in view of the proposed celebration of a religious marriage service. In some exceptional circumstances (e.g., certain Catholic-Jewish marriages) it may be necessary that the dispensation be granted so that a civil ceremony may be performed. In any case, a public form that is civilly recognized for the celebration of marriage is required.

● *Recording Marriages (M.P., No. 10)*

12. In a mixed marriage for which there has been granted a dispensation from the canonical form, an ecclesiastical record of the marriage shall be kept in the chancery of the diocese which granted the dispensation from the impediment, and in the marriage records of the parish from which application for the dispensation was made.

13. It is the responsibility of the priest who submits the request for the dispensation to see that, after the public form of marriage ceremony is performed, notices of the marriage are sent in the usual form to: (a) the parish and chancery noted above (12); (b) the place of baptism of the Catholic party.

The recording of other mixed marriages is not changed.

● *Celebration of Marriages Between Catholics and Non-Catholics*

14. It is not permitted to have two religious marriage services or to have a single service in which both the Catholic marriage ritual and a non-Catholic marriage ritual are celebrated jointly or successively (cf. *Matrimonia Mixta,* No. 13).

15. With the permission of the local ordinary and the consent of the appropriate authority of the other church or community, a non-Catholic minister may be invited to participate in the Catholic marriage service by giving additional prayers, blessings, or words of greeting and exhortation. If the marriage is not part of the Eucharisic celebration, the minister may also be invited to read a lesson and/or to preach (cf. *Ecumenical Directory,* Part I, No. 56).

16. In the case where there has been a dispensation from the Catholic canonical form and the priest has been invited to participate in the non-Catholic marriage service, with the permission of the local ordinary and the consent of the appropriate authority of the other church or communion, he may do so by giving additional prayers, blessings, or words of greeting and exhortation. If the marriage service is not part

of the Lord's Supper or the principal liturgical service of the Word, the priest, if invited, may also read a lesson and/or preach (cf. *ibid.*).

17. To the extent that Eucharistic sharing is not permitted by the general discipline of the Church (cf. *Matrimonia Mixta,* No. 11, and the exceptions in No. 39 of the *Ecumenical Directory,* Part I, May 14, 1967), this is to be considered when plans are being made to have the mixed marriage at Mass or not.

18. Since the revised Catholic rite of marriage includes a rich variety of scriptural readings and biblically oriented prayers and blessings from which to choose, its use may promote harmony and unity on the occasion of a mixed marriage (cf. *Introduction to the Rite of Marriage,* No. 9), provided the service is carefully planned and celebrated. The general directives that the selection of texts and other preparations should involve "all concerned, including the faithful . . ." (*General Instructions of the Roman Missal,* No. 73; cf. No. 313) are especially applicable to the mixed marriage service, where the concerns of the couple, the non-Catholic minister and other participants should be considered.

• *Place of Marriage*

19. The ordinary place of marriage is in the parish church or other sacred place. For serious reasons, the local ordinary may permit the celebration of a mixed marriage, when there has been no dispensation from the canonical form and the Catholic marriage service is to be celebrated, outside a Catholic church or chapel, providing there is no scandal involved and proper delegation is granted (for example, where there is no Catholic church in the area, etc.).

20. If there has been a dispensation from canonical form, ordinarily the marriage service is celebrated in the non-Catholic church.

• *Conclusion*

The practical forms for the implementation of the directives on the local level are to be developed by the local chancery in accordance with its normal practices.

The provisions of this document, as well as the apostolic letter upon which it is based, call for a renewed pastoral concern toward couples contemplating and those already in mixed marriages.

We urge all who are in any way engaged in the pastoral ministry to families to study this and related documents, and sensitively to apply these latest provisions.

To assist our priests, Religious and lay people in carrying out the further implementation of this document, we [the NCCB] pledge a cooperative effort on the part of appropriate agencies of the National Conference of Catholic Bishops and the United States Catholic Conference. Specifically, we call upon:

• The Family Life Division of the United States Catholic Conference to develop basic pre-marriage and marriage education programs incorporating the norms and spirit of this document.

• The Bishops' Committee for Ecumenical and Interreligious Affairs and the Bishops' Committee on the Liturgy to explore the possibility of an ecumenical form for mixed marriage. This should be done with appropriate consultation involving interested churches and ecclesial communities separated from us.

• The Bishops' Committee on Priestly Formation to develop a plan of study and renewal for the pastoral care of mixed marriages to be imparted both through seminary education and through programs for the continuing education of clergy.

While much remains to be done if the Church is to exercise more adequately a proper pastoral solicitude for couples in mixed marriages, we take this opportunity to commend the countless persons, lay, Religious and clergy, at the diocesan and parish level, who are engaged in marriage education and family counseling throughout the country.

Finally, we encourage the priests of the United States, who share with us a particular responsibility for the Church's ministry, to renew their pastoral solicitude for couples already joined in a mixed marriage, and also for those engaged couples of differing religious convictions who will soon begin married life together.

8

Exposition of the Blessed Sacrament

Relationship Between Exposition and Mass

Exposition of the Holy Eucharist, either in the ciborium or in the monstrance, is intended to acknowledge Christ's marvelous presence in the sacrament. Exposition invites us to the spiritual union with him that culminates in sacramental Communion. Thus it fosters very well the worship which is due to Christ in spirit and in truth.

This kind of exposition must clearly express the cult of the Blessed Sacrament in its relationship to the Mass. The plan of the exposition should carefully avoid anything which might somehow obscure the principal desire of Christ in instituting the Eucharist, namely, to be with us as food, medicine and comfort.

During the exposition of the Blessed Sacrament, the celebration of Mass is prohibited in the body of the Church. The celebration of Mass reveals in its orderly progress the various ways in which Christ is present in the Church. He is present in the congregation which gathers to acknowledge him; present in his word during the reading of Scripture and the homily; present in the person of the minister; last but not least, present under the form of bread and wine. His presence as God and man in the sacrament of the Eucharist is without parallel elsewhere: he is wholly and completely present. This is not to deny that Christ is genuinely present in other ways too, but we describe this as the Real Presence "because it is the most personal." In addition to these reasons, the celebration of the Eucharistic mystery includes in a more perfect way the internal communion to which exposition seeks to lead the faithful.

If exposition of the Blessed Sacrament is extended for an entire day or over several days, it is to be interrupted during the celebration of Mass. Mass may be celebrated in a chapel distinct from the area of exposition if at least some members of the faithful remain in adoration.

Regulations for Exposition

A single genuflection is made in the presence of the Blessed Sacrament, whether reserved in the tabernacle or exposed for public adoration.

For exposition of the Blessed Sacrament in the monstrance, four to six candles are lighted, as at Mass, and incense is used. For exposition of the Blessed Sacrament in the ciborium, at least two candles should be lighted, and incense may be used.

• *Lengthy Exposition*

In churches where the Eucharist is regularly reserved, it is recommended that solemn exposition of the Blessed Sacrament for an extended period of time should take place once a year, even though this period is not strictly continuous. In this way the local community may reflect more profoundly upon this mystery and adore Christ in the sacrament.

This kind of exposition, however, may take place, with the consent of the local ordinary, only if suitable numbers of the faithful are expected to be present.

For a grave and general necessity the local ordinary may direct that a more extended period of supplication before the Blessed Sacrament exposed take place in churches where the faithful assemble in large numbers.

If a period of uninterrupted exposition is not possible, because of too few worshipers, the Blessed Sacrament may be replaced in the tabernacle during periods which have been scheduled and announced beforehand. This reposition may not take place more often than twice during the day, for example, about noon and at night.

The following form of simple reposition may be observed: the priest or deacon, vested in an alb, or surplice over a cassock, and a stole, replaces the Blessed Sacrament in the tabernacle after a brief period of adoration and a prayer said with those present. The exposition of the Blessed Sacrament may take place in the same manner (at the scheduled time).

• *Brief Period of Exposition*

Shorter expositions of the Eucharist are to be arranged in such a way that the blessing with the Eucharist is preceded by a suitable period for readings of the word of God, songs, prayers and sufficient time for silent prayer.

Exposition which is held exclusively for the giving of benediction is prohibited.

• *Adoration in Religious Communities*

According to the constitutions and regulations of their institute, some Religious communities and other groups have the practice of perpetual Eucharistic adoration or adoration over extended periods of time. It is strongly recommended that they pattern this holy practice in harmony with the spirit of the liturgy. Thus, when the whole community takes part in adoration before Christ the Lord, readings, songs and religious silence may foster effectively the spiritual life of the community. This will promote among the members of the Religious house the spirit of unity and brotherhood which the Eucharist signifies and effects, and the cult of the sacrament may express a noble form of worship.

The form of adoration in which one or two members of the community take turns before the Blessed Sacrament is also to be maintained and is highly commended. In accordance with the life of the institute, as approved by the Church, the worshipers adore Christ the Lord in the sacrament and pray to him in the name of the whole community and of the Church.

The Minister of Exposition

The ordinary minister for exposition of the Eucharist is a priest or deacon. At the end of the period of adoration, before the reposition, he blesses the people with the sacrament.

In the absence of a priest or deacon or if they are lawfully impeded, the following persons may publicly expose and later repose the Holy Eucharist for the adoration of the faithful: (a) an acolyte or special minister of Communion; (b) a member of a Religious community or of a lay association of men or women which is devoted to Eucharistic adoration, upon appointment by the local ordinary.

Such ministers may open the tabernacle and also, if suitable, place the ciborium on the altar or place the host in the monstrance. At the end of the period of adoration, they replace the Blessed Sacrament in the tabernacle. It is not lawful, however, for them to give the blessing with the sacrament.

The minister, if he is a priest or deacon, should vest in an alb or in a surplice over a cassock and should wear a white stole.

Other ministers should wear either the liturgical vestments which are usual in the region or the vesture which is suitable for this ministry and which has been approved by the ordinary.

The priest or deacon should wear a white cope and humeral veil to give the blessing at the end of adoration, when the exposition takes place with the monstrance; in the case of exposition in the ciborium, the humeral veil should be worn.

Rite of Eucharistic Exposition and Benediction

• *Exposition*

After the people have assembled, a song may be sung while the minister comes to the altar. If the Holy Eucharist is not reserved at the altar where the exposition is to take place, the minister puts on a humeral veil and brings the sacrament from the place of reservation; he is accompanied by servers or by the faithful with lighted candles.

The ciborium or monstrance should be placed upon the table of the altar which is covered with a cloth. If exposition with the monstrance is to extend over a long period, a throne in an elevated position may be used, but this should not be too lofty or distant. After exposition, if the monstrance is used, the minister incenses the sacrament. If the adoration is to be lengthy, he may then withdraw.

In the case of a more solemn and lengthy exposition, the host should be consecrated in the Mass which immediately precedes the exposition and after Communion should be placed in the monstrance upon the altar. The Mass ends with the prayer after Communion, and the concluding rites are omitted. Before the priest leaves, he may place the Blessed Sacrament on the throne and incense it.

• *Adoration*

During the exposition there should be prayers, songs and readings to direct the attention of the faithful to the worship of Christ the Lord.

To encourage a prayerful spirit, there should be readings from Scripture with a homily or brief exhortations to develop a better understanding of the Eucharistic mystery. It is also desirable for the people to respond to the word of God by singing and to spend some periods of time in religious silence.

Part of the Liturgy of the Hours, especially the principal hours, may be celebrated before the Blessed Sacrament when there is a lengthy period of exposition. This liturgy extends the praise and thanksgiving offered to God in the Eucharistic celebration to the several hours of the day; it directs the prayers of the Church to Christ and through him to the Father in the name of the whole world.

• *Benediction*

Toward the end of the exposition the priest or deacon goes to the altar, genuflects and kneels. Then a hymn or other Eucharistic song is sung. Meanwhile the minister, while kneeling, incenses the sacrament if the exposition has taken place with the monstrance.

Afterward the minister rises and sings or says:

Let us pray.

After a brief period of silence, the minister continues:

Lord Jesus Christ,
you gave us the eucharist
as the memorial of your suffering and death.
May our worship of this sacrament of your body and
blood

help us to experience the salvation you won for us
and the peace of the kingdom
where you live with the Father and the Holy Spirit,
one God, for ever and ever.

All respond:

Amen.

Other prayers may be chosen:

**Lord our God,
in this great sacrament
we come into the presence of Jesus Christ, your Son,
born of the Virgin Mary
and crucified for our salvation.
May we who declare our faith in this fountain of love
          and mercy
drink from it the water of everlasting life.
We ask this through Christ our Lord.**

Or:

**Lord our God,
may we always give due honor
to the sacramental presence of the Lamb who was
          slain for us.
May our faith be rewarded
by the vision of his glory,
who lives and reigns for ever and ever.**

Or:

**Lord our God,
you have given us the true bread from heaven.
In the strength of this food
may we live always by your life
and rise in glory on the last day.
We ask this through Christ our Lord.**

Or:

Lord,

give to our hearts
the light of faith and the fire of love,
that we may worship in spirit and in truth
our God and Lord, present in this sacrament,
who lives and reigns for ever and ever.

Or:

Lord,
may this sacrament of new life
warm our hearts with your love
and make us eager
for the eternal joy of your kingdom.
We ask this through Christ our Lord.

Or:

Lord our God,
teach us to cherish in our hearts
the paschal mystery of your Son
by which you redeemed the world.
Watch over the gifts of grace
your love has given us
and bring them to fulfillment
in the glory of heaven.
We ask this through Christ our Lord.

After the prayer the priest or deacon puts on the humeral veil, genuflects and takes the monstrance or ciborium. He makes the sign of the cross over the people with the monstrance or ciborium, in silence.

• *Reposition*

After the blessing the priest or deacon who gave the blessing, or another priest or deacon, replaces the Blessed Sacrament in the tabernacle and genuflects. Meanwhile the people may sing or say an acclamation, and the minister then leaves.

Hymns

PANGE LINGUA

Sing, my tongue, the Savior's glory,	Pange, lingua, gloriosi

130

Of his flesh the mystery sing:
Of the blood, all price exceeding,
Shed by our immortal King,
Destined, for the world's redemp-
tion,
From a noble womb to spring.

Of a pure and spotless Virgin
Born for us on earth below,
He, as man, with man conversing,
Stayed, the seeds of truth to sow;
Then he closed in solemn order
Wondrously his life of woe.

On the night of that Last Supper
Seated with his chosen band,
He, the paschal victim eating,
First fulfills the law's command;
Then as food to his apostles
Gives himself with his own hand.

Word made flesh, the bread of na-
ture
by his word to flesh he turns;
Wine into his blood he changes:
What though sense no change dis-
cerns?
Only be the heart in earnest,
Faith her lesson quickly learns.
Amen.

Corporis mysterium
Sanguinisque pretiosi
Quem in mundi pretium,
Fructus ventris generosi,

Rex effudit gentium.

Nobis datus, nobis natus
Ex intacta Virgine,
Et in mundo conversatus,
Sparso verbi semine,
Sui moras incolatus
Miro clausit ordine.

In supremae nocte coenae
Recumbens cum fratribus,
Observata lege plene
Cibis in legalibus,
Cibum turbae duodenae
Se dat suis manibus.

Verbum caro, panem verum,

Verbo carem efficit,
Fitque sanguis Christi merum;
Et si sensus deficit,

Ad firmandum cor sincerum
Sola fides sufficit. Amen.

TANTUM ERGO

Down in adoration falling,
Lo! the sacred host we hail;
Lo! o'er ancient forms departing,
Newer rites of grace prevail;
Faith for all defects supplying,
Where the feeble senses fail.

To the everlasting Father
And the Son who reigns on high,
With the Holy Ghost proceeding
Forth from each eternally,
Be salvation, honor, blessing,

Tantum ergo sacramentum
Veneremur cernui:
Et antiquum documentum
Novo cedat ritue:
Praestet fides supplementum
Sensuum defectui.

Genitori Genitoque
Laus et jubilatio
Salus, honor, virtus quoque
Sit, et benedictio:
Procedenti ab utroque

Might and endless majesty. Amen.

Compar sit laudatio. Amen.

V. You send them bread from heaven. (Alleluia.)

R. Having in itself every delight. (Allelulia.)

Let us pray.

O God, who under this wonderful sacrament has left us a memorial of your passion: grant, we beseech you, so to reverence the sacred mysteries of your body and blood, that we may ever feel within ourselves the fruit of your redemption. Who live and reign forever and ever. Amen.

V. Panem de caelo praestitisti eis. (Alleluja.)

R. Omne delectamentum in se habentem. (Alleluja.)

Oremus.

Deus, qui nobis sub sacramento mirabili passionis tuae memoriam reliquisti; tribue, quaesumus, ita nos corporis et sanguinis tui sacra mysteria venerari, ut redemptionis tuae fructum in nobis jugiter sentiamus. Qui vivis et regnas in saecula saeculorum. Amen.

O SACRUM CONVIVIUM

O blessed feast in which Christ is received: the sacred memory of the passion is celebrated; the mind is filled with grace and a foretaste of future glory is given us!

O sacrum convivium, in quo Christus sumitur: recolitur memoria passionis ejus; mens impletur gratia; et futurae gloriae nobis pignus datur.

AVE VERUM

Hail to thee, true body, sprung
From the Virgin Mary's womb:
The same that on the cross was hung
And bore for man the bitter doom!

Thou, whose side was pierced and flowed
Both with water and with blood,
Suffer us to taste of thee
In our life's last agony,
Son of Mary! Jesus blest! Sweetest, gentlest, holiest!

Ave verum corpus natum de Maria virgine:
Vere passum, immolatum in cruce pro homine;

Cujus latus, perforatum, fluxit aqua et sanguine.
Esto nobis praegustatum mortis in examine.

O Jesu dulcis; O Jesu pie; O Jesu, Fili Mariae!

Meditation

God's union with us is his gift to us. So our union with one another is conditioned by the act of giving. We are members of Christ. But to keep this place of privilege we have to give and keep giving. Sacrifice is the law of love, both human and divine.

God's love, then, is to be given out with both hands, communicating to others the good things of Jesus Christ — this we do when we love one another. In this setting of love we come before the Blessed Sacrament.

The love of Christ has gathered us together.
Let us rejoice in him and be cheerful;
Let us love the living God,
And love each other with honest hearts.
Let us take care not to be isolated in ourselves;
Let ill will, quarrels and disagreements stop,
And Christ our Lord be among us.

At the Last Supper, our Lord identified himself completely with this command of loving one another. He said: "This is *my* commandment." The Church assumes, when a Christian comes to worship, that love of neighbor and reconciliation with one's brothers is a fact. Our Lord himself told his hearers that love of one another was the condition for making an offering at the altar. He taught that if we had anything against our neighbor, we should first go back and be reconciled, and then come before the Lord to offer the gift of sacrifice.

In the Eucharist we have the sacrament of love. It is here before the altar that we can interpret best the true concept of love of all men in Christ. It is here before Christ, transfigured in the joy of the resurrection, that the most crucial test of love is experienced.

Nor race, nor creed can love exclude
If honored by God's name.
Our brotherhood embraces all
Whose Father is the same.

Prayers

ACT OF TRUST

"We can never make an end of our gratitude to thee, who never ceasest to cherish us with thy mercy. Who can sufficiently praise the works of thy power, thou whose divine presence no human eye can see, whose greatness no words can tell? Let it be sufficient, then, that we are able to love thee as our Father, reverence thee as our Ruler, acknowledge thee as our Creator, welcome thee as our Redeemer. So as most gentle Ruler and Guide, lead us on that narrow path that thou wouldst have us ascend to the attainment of our lasting happiness" (*Gothic Missal, seventh century*).

133

ACT OF HUMILITY

"Devoutly kneeling before thy Majesty, we earnestly pray that, since thou dost see the limits of our human weakness, thou wouldst not in anger blame us for our disobedience, but with thy boundless pity cleanse us, teach us and comfort us; and since, if thou dost not help us, we cannot do what is well-pleasing in thy sight, let thy grace come to help us, that we may live to our own well-being, ever friends with thee" *(Eleventh-century Missal)*.

PRAYERS FOR OTHERS

• "O Lord God of strength, who are true charity, unshaken tranquillity and hope unfailing: do thou, O Lord our God, give to thy servants here present in the sight of thy Majesty, the gifts of charity, kindness, calmness and lasting peace, that we may all in purity of heart and goodness of soul have peace with each other" *(Liturgy of St. John)*.

• "Be mindful, O Lord, of all those who have asked us to remember them in the prayers and petitions we now make in thy sight. O Lord our God, be mindful of those whose memory is always with us, and those who are especially in our thoughts at this moment and in our present prayer. Bring them the grace of a strong and lasting defense against all that may harm them" *(Coptic Liturgy)*.

PRAYERS FOR THE LOVE OF GOD

• "A man will have a great and long struggle with himself, before he fully learns to master self and to turn his whole affection towards God.

"When a man relies on himself, he easily turns aside to human consolations. But a true lover of Christ, and a diligent pursuer of virtue, does not fall back upon consolations, nor seek such sensible sweetnesses; he prefers hard trials and would wish to undergo severe labors for Christ" *(Imitation of Christ)*.

• "O my Lord Jesus, let me never for an instant forget that thou hast established on earth a kingdom of thy own; that the Church is thy work, thy establishment, thy instrument; that we are under thy rule; that where the Church speaks, thou dost speak. Let not familiarity with this wonderful truth lead me to be insensible to it" *(John Henry Newman)*.

• "O Christ our Lord, perfect lover of mankind, grant, we beseech thee, that there may ever abide in us, knowledge, intelligence, understanding and wisdom. So may we see ever deeper and deeper, and understand and appreciate the lesson of thy holiness, which is open before us in thy sight. As thou didst so enrich Paul, making him worthy of such great graces, make us also, we beseech thee, O Author of life, to imitate him and follow closely in his footsteps" *(Missa Ethiopum, tenth century)*.

Lord, have mercy on us.
Christ, have mercy on us.
Lord, have mercy on us.
Christ, hear us.
Christ, graciously hear us.
God the Father of heaven, *have mercy on us.*

[After each invocation, respond with: *Have mercy on us.*]

God the Son, Redeemer of the world,
God the Holy Spirit,
Holy Trinity, one God,
Heart of Jesus, Son of the eternal Father,
Heart of Jesus, formed by the Holy Spirit in the Virgin's womb,
Heart of Jesus, hypostatically united to the Word of God,
Heart of Jesus, infinite in majesty,
Heart of Jesus, God's holy temple,
Heart of Jesus, tabernacle of the Most High,
Heart of Jesus, house of God and gate of heaven,
Heart of Jesus, glowing furnace of charity,
Heart of Jesus, vessel of love and justice,
Heart of Jesus, full of loving kindness,
Heart of Jesus, deep well of all virtues,
Heart of Jesus, most worthy of all praise,
Heart of Jesus, royal home of all hearts,
Heart of Jesus, treasure-house of wisdom and knowledge,
Heart of Jesus, wherein abides all the fullness of the Godhead,
Heart of Jesus, in which the Father is well pleased,
Heart of Jesus, of whose fullness we have all received,
Heart of Jesus, desire of the eternal hills,
Heart of Jesus, patient and rich in mercy,
Heart of Jesus, bountiful to all who call upon you,
Heart of Jesus, fount of life and holiness,
Heart of Jesus, propitiation for our offenses,
Heart of Jesus, overwhelmed with reproaches,
Heart of Jesus, bruised for our iniquities,
Heart of Jesus, patient even unto death,
Heart of Jesus, opened by a spear,
Heart of Jesus, fountain of all consolation,
Heart of Jesus, our life and resurrection,
Heart of Jesus, our peace and atonement,
Heart of Jesus, victim of all our sins,
Heart of Jesus, health of them that trust in you,
Heart of Jesus, hope of them that die in you,
Heart of Jesus, delight of all the saints,
Lamb of God, you take away the sins of the world: *spare us, O Lord.*

Lamb of God, you take away the sins of the world: *graciously hear us, O Lord.*

Lamb of God, you take away the sins of the world: *have mercy on us.*

V. Jesus, meek and humble of heart.
R. Make our hearts like unto yours.

Let us pray.

Almighty and everlasting God, look upon the heart of your well-beloved Son, honoring you and making amends in the name of sinners and whereas they implore your pity, do you mercifully grant forgiveness, in the name of your Son, Jesus Christ, who lives and reigns with you for ever and ever. Amen.

EUCHARISTIC CONGRESS PRAYER

Father in heaven,
You have made us for yourself;
Our hearts are restless until they rest in you.
Fulfill this longing through Jesus, the bread of life,
So that we may witness to him
Who alone satisfies the hungers of the human family.
By the power of your Spirit
Lead us to the heavenly table
Where we may feast on the vision of your glory
For ever and ever. Amen.

Eucharistic Day or Holy Hour

The Sacred Congregation for the Sacraments and Divine Worship has stated that exposition of the Blessed Sacrament stimulates the people of God to a deeper awareness of the Real Presence of Christ and encourages parishes to have each year a period of solemn exposition in order to give the faithful an opportunity of adoring and meditating on the Eucharistic mystery with deeper devotion. Care must be taken that this worship is seen in relationship to the Mass.

It is forbidden to celebrate Mass in the presence of the Blessed Sacrament exposed. During the exposition, Mass may not be celebrated in the same area of the church. The day or period of exposition could well begin with Mass and, if permitted, a votive Mass of the Eucharist. At the conclusion of the Mass, exposition takes place.

Suggested Readings

- Proverbs 10:1-6.
- Acts 2:42-47.

- Acts 10:34, 37-43.
- 1 Corinthians 11:23-26.
- Hebrews 9:11-15.
- Mark 14:12-16, 22-26.
- Luke 24:13-35.
- John 6:24-35.
- John 6:41-51.
- John 6:52-58.
- Psalm 23:1-6.
- Psalm 34:2-11.
- Psalms 130, 145, 147, 148, 149 and 150.
- *Prefaces:* Preface of the Holy Eucharist I (P-47); Preface of the Holy Eucharist II (P-48); Preface of Christ the King (P-51).

9

Prayers When Visiting the Sick

For Hospital Patients in General

Father, I thank you for raising up doctors, nurses and all medical teams, and for placing me in this great country of ours where these are available. Naturally, I do not want to be in this hospital, but help me to see a blessing in this. Heal me not only in body but also in mind and soul so that I may be the kind of person you want me to be. Amen.

Jesus, you healed many patients. Bless my doctors, nurses and everyone who cares for me with your own wisdom, understanding, gentleness and respect for personhood and pour your healing power into them. May we all cooperate for your honor and glory. Amen.

Holy Spirit, you made your dwelling in me through baptism and confirmation. I shall feel lonely and awkward in this place. Warm and strengthen my heart with your love and friendship that I may truly realize the saying that the Holy Spirit hovers over the pillow of every patient. Amen.

For those whom I have left at home [*here name your friends*], that they may be surrounded by God's love and care and their anxiety lightened with his heavenly peace, I pray to the Father . . .
For my fellow patients, that we may grow in some kind of community of love and understanding together, I pray to the Father . . .
For the chaplains in this hospital, that they may be anointed with Jesus' power, I pray to the Father . . .
For the laboratory technicians, radiologists, physical therapists and all other workers in this hospital, that they may realize the dignity of their calling in Christ's ministry of healing, I pray to the Father. Amen.

Father, when we are stripped of our clothes, and others handle our bodies, we feel the loss of the dignity of personhood. Please give me the grace to accept these humiliations with poise and a sense of elegant humor in union with the dispositions of your beloved Son when he hung naked on the cross and the crowds passed by, jeering at him. My suffer-

139

ing is nothing compared with Jesus' or with those who endure imprisonment or extreme poverty even nowadays; yet grant, if it is your will, that the people who care for me may, by your clemency, treat me as they would like to be treated themselves and thus fulfill your Son's precept, "You shall love your neighbor as yourself." Amen.

Mother Mary, you watched the suffering and embarrassment of your only Son. Be the mainstay and support of my friends and relatives who endure mental anguish because I can no longer attend to my own needs. Pray to the Father to give them not only that same sense of warm care and awestruck love that must have been yours when first you lifted the Son of God, a naked, helpless babe, into your arms, but also your respect for his adult manhood when you saw him naked on the cross. Amen.

Lord, I cry out in anguish of soul and I ask for rest. Lord, take away despair and grant me peace of mind and body. Grant me blessed sleep. But if this is not your gracious will, I unite myself to your Son's sleepless vigil in Gethsemane and with him I say, "Father, not my will but yours." Amen.

Lord, even as, alone, Jacob fought throughout the night with the angel and thereafter received a blessing, that is, the transmission of divine vitality, bless me, also alone, this long, long night. I seem to have no rest for my body, but I ask you to grant some benefit to my soul. Amen.

Father, thank you for the medicine which brings sleep. May I and my fellow patients have rest of body. Even as you dealt kindly with your servant Jacob, fill this hospital with a sense of your vivid presence that the wondrous fragrance of your love may never leave us. Through Christ our Lord. Amen.

Lord, our God and gracious Father, while the angels and saints give you ceaseless praise, you give to your loved ones on earth the sacred hours of sleep. May these hours be hallowed as your name is hallowed; may they refresh our bodies, minds and souls; may they draw a quiet curtain over all our weaknesses and sins, and prove to be the gateway to a new day. Amen.

Jesus, tonight some soul will glide from this mortal earth to the many mansions you have prepared for those who love you. Grant that he may be surrounded by his loved ones, without pain of body, with clarity and serenity of mind, and with joyful expectancy of soul. Amen.

For Patients With Eye Disorders

Scriptural Reading (Mark 10:46-52)

They came to Jericho next, and as he was leaving that place with his disciples and a sizable crowd, there was a blind beggar Bartimaeus ("son of Timaeus") sitting by the roadside. On hearing that it was Jesus of Nazareth, he began to call out, "Jesus, Son of David, have pity on me!" Many people were scolding him to make him keep quiet, but he shouted all the louder, "Son of David, have pity on me!" Then Jesus stopped and said, "Call him over." So they called the blind man over, telling him as they did so, "You have nothing to fear from him! Get up! He is calling you!" He threw aside his cloak, jumped up and came to Jesus. Jesus asked him, "What do you want me to do for you?" "Rabboni," the blind man said, "I want to see." Jesus said in reply, "Be on your way! Your faith has healed you." Immediately he received his sight and started to follow him up the road.

Prayers

Jesus, my Lord and my brother, you preached more eloquently from the cross than during your busy charismatic ministry because you preached the greatest love — namely, the innocent dying for the guilty. You allowed Paul to be imprisoned, but the gospel was not chained. You let the blood of the martyrs be the life-force of the Church. Teach me to witness to you even from my hospital bed. Give me the wisdom and grace to help my fellow patients, my visitors, and even the staff. Show me that I am not useless but that "a door has been opened wide for my work . . ." (1 Corinthians 16:9). Even though there are many adversities, give me resourcefulness to overcome these. Amen.

Father, hear my complaints with a sympathetic ear as you have heard the complaints of stricken men and women, even psalmists, prophets and saints, throughout the years. If it is your will, let this chalice pass from me and from my relatives and friends. Let me now read, learn and inwardly digest your answer to Job so that in some small way I may comprehend the marvelous and unfathomable mystery of your love and purpose for us all. Amen.

Lord, in my misery I acknowledge, even though it is with an effort, your superior wisdom and providence. As you guide the whole universe so tenderly and with such expertise, so now guide me and my family through this experience. Let me feel the power of your loving presence. Amen.

Heavenly Father, Jesus my brother, and Holy Spirit, St. Paul's words express my feelings so well. In one way I long to remain on this earth; in another I look forward to the end of pain and illness and I long

141

for the felicity of heaven, to be with you, my Triune God. Teach me now how to go forth with dignity, serenity, joy and expectancy and yet not to be heedless of the grief of my friends. Grant them the grace to rejoice that I shall be with you; give them understanding into the wondrous mystery of the communion of the saints and let Mary and the companions who stood with her by the cross be with us all. Amen.

For Persons in Danger of Death

(The sense of hearing is the last to leave a dying person. Even though the dying person cannot respond, he often hears what is said.)

Jesu, Maria — I am near to death,
And thou art calling me; I know it now,
Not by the token of this faltering breath,
This chill at heart, this dampness on my brow —
(Jesu, have mercy! Mary, pray for me!)
'Tis this new feeling never felt before,
(Be with me, Lord, in my extremity!)
That I am going, that I am no more.
'Tis this strange innermost abandonment,
(Lover of souls! Great God! I look to thee!)
This emptying out of each constituent
And natural force, by which I come to be.
Pray for me, O my friends; a visitant
Is knocking his dire summons at my door,
The like of whom, to scare me and to daunt,
Has never, never come to me before:
So pray for me, my friends, who have not strength to pray.

— *John Henry Newman*

Abide with me; fast falls the eventide;
The darkness deepens; Lord, with me abide;
When other helpers fail, and comforts flee,
Help of the helpless, O abide with me.
Swift to its close ebbs out life's little day;
Earth's joys grow dim, its glories pass away;
Change and decay in all around I see;
O thou who changest not, abide with me.
Hold thou thy cross before my closing eyes;
Shine through the gloom, and point me to the skies;
Heaven's morning breaks, and earth's vain shadows flee;
In life, in death, O Lord, abide with me.

— *Henry Francis Lyte*

Lead, kindly Light, amid the encircling gloom,
Lead thou me on;
The night is dark and I am far from home,
Lead thou me on.
Keep thou my feet; I do not ask to see
The distant scene; one step enough for me.
I was not ever thus, nor prayed that thou
Shouldst lead me on;
I loved to choose and see my path; but now
Lead thou me on.
I loved the garish day, and, spite of fears,
Pride ruled my will: remember not past years.
So long thy power hath blest me, sure it still
Will lead me on
O'er moor and fen, o'er crag and torrent, till
The night is gone,
And with the morn those angel faces smile,
Which I have loved long since and lost awhile.

— *John Henry Newman*

Traditional Prayers

ACT OF FAITH

O my God, I believe that you are one God in three divine persons: Father, Son and Holy Spirit. I believe that your divine Son became man and died for our sins, and that he will come to judge the living and the dead. I believe these and all the truths that the Catholic Church teaches, because you have revealed them, who can neither deceive nor be deceived. Amen.

ACT OF HOPE

O my God, relying on your almighty power and infinite mercy and promises, I hope to obtain pardon of my sins, the help of your grace and life everlasting through the merits of Jesus Christ, my Lord and Redeemer. Amen.

ACT OF LOVE

O my God, I love you above all things with my whole heart and soul, because you are all good and worthy of all love. I love my neighbor as myself for the love of you. I forgive all who have injured me, and ask pardon of all whom I have injured. Amen.

ACT OF CONTRITION

O my God, I am heartily sorry for having offended you, and I detest all my sins, because of your just punishments, but most of all because they offend you, my God, who are all good and deserving of all love. I firmly resolve, with the help of your grace, to sin no more and to avoid the near occasions of sin. Amen.

ACT OF RESIGNATION TO DEATH

O Lord, my God, from this day I accept from your hand willingly and with submission the kind of death that it may please you to send me, with all its sorrows, pains and anguish. Amen.

Suggested Readings

- Sirach 38:9-14.
- Psalm 16.
- Psalm 18:1-16.
- Job 7:11-16.
- John 14:1-7.

10

Rite of Anointing

A Pastoral Commentary

The question facing those involved in parish ministry is: "How can we best instruct the faithful concerning the implementation of changes in 'extreme unction'?" Or perhaps: "How can we give this rite a better pastoral-liturgical expression in our particular parish?" The following are a few possible suggestions.

The question — "How can the sacrament of the anointing of the sick find a better pastoral-liturgical expression in the parish?" — is in the first instance a catechetical one. Renewal in any area of sacramental life must begin with a balanced educational presentation. This enables the people to better grasp the reason for change and assists them in appreciating the historical continuity that a sacrament holds throughout the ages. People are not unwilling to change; on the contrary they look to change and renewal for growth and strength. Updating helps people to cope adequately with the evolving world around them.

Nothing, absolutely nothing, destroys more effectively than ignorance. Ignorance, which results from lack of information (offered by competent authority) and integration, breeds fear and distrust, the enemies of renewal. Therefore, if we are to avoid a crisis of ignorance within the Church's sacramental life, then catechesis becomes our categorial imperative. This is especially true in relation to the anointing of the sick. The reason for our special educational need in this area stems from the hard fact that little knowledge of this sacrament has filtered down through the ranks of the faithful. A second cause is emotional in nature. Anointing of the sick deals with people at a highly emotional time in their lives. Therefore, caution is required if we hope to avoid hard feelings. Countless believers have, in the past, been anointed only when in danger of death or when they appeared to be dead (conditional administration). To reverse this position without a patient catechesis would be a disservice to the Church. One of the grave errors of the post-Vatican II Church is that we have asked people to move ahead without ensuring that they knew why they were to do so.

Primarily, one must begin the process of renewal by convincing the people that this sacrament of the anointing is not a sacrament for the dead or dying or even merely the gravely ill (unto death), but essentially a sacrament for the sick. Once this transition is accomplished the sailing will be relatively clear.

Secondly, one must help the people to come to a better understanding of the effect of the sacrament. The desired effect and the actual effect is not merely to heal the soul (spiritual effect), nor merely to heal the body (physical effect), but a blending of the two. The whole person is somehow healed. The people should be exhorted not to look for either effect exclusive from the other, but somehow believe that the sacramental effect is a graced event affecting the whole person.

Thirdly, the faithful must be instructed so as to see the sacrament for what it truly is: a sacrament of faith and hope. Sickness provides a temptation to despair in the Lord, to cry out in Job-like fashion — "My God, my God, why have you forsaken me?" Sickness creates the tendency toward selfishness, toward self-pity which makes the sick person feel: "I'm the only one in the world with any kind of trouble," or "My trouble is at least worse than others' troubles." This concentration on the "me" and "my" illness initiates the temptation to disbelieve in "Yahweh's mighty hand and outstretched arm and his signs and wonders." Likewise, sickness provides the occasion whereby many fail at prayer. The sick often give up praying. Sickness in general poses a threat to the sick person's faith in God.

What does the anointing of the sick do? From what we know from Scripture and the tradition of the Church regarding the administration of this sacrament, we can say with certitude that a major effect of the sacrament of anointing is some sort of faith expansion (which also may be the cause of physical healing). The sacrament is one of faith. It inspires confidence within a person's mind and heart. This is a psychological effect of sorts and could produce a physical effect. Medical science informs us that one of the essentials to true healing is a person's attitude, that is, his will to live. It is likely therefore that the faith, which anointing inspires, can and often does produce a visible healing effect.

The final ingredient for true renewal of the sacrament of anointing lies within ecclesiology. The ecclesial dimension of the sacrament is essential to proper renewal. This dimension must be promoted and emphasized. Without it the sacrament of the anointing of the sick is rendered shallow and, in a sense, incomprehensible.

It has been stressed, especially since the close of the Second Vatican Council, that baptism draws us into a relationship with every other Christian. By virtue of this sacrament an ecclesial dimension (a social or communal dimension) of sacramentality is established. We are no longer mere individual believers, detached from or independent of a community, but are members of a Church (people of God) and as such offer praise, thanksgiving and acts of worship together with others in one, true communal enterprise. We are brothers and therefore definitely related. The Eucharist strengthens this fellowship for it is the sacrament of unity and the bond of charity.

Therefore, when one of the members of this ecclesial family falls sick all are somehow affected. Everyone is concerned with the welfare of this particular individual; blood is thicker than water and we all have the blood of Christ running through our veins.

Christ established through his Church a vehicle for our response in the sacrament of the anointing of the sick. Herein lies a graced event; an encounter with the Lord of history and the Lord of our lives. The sacraments are signs of the risen Lord; the sacraments are the sacred signs of the Church; the sacraments are our signs, our means of responding in a most efficacious way to those who have fallen ill.

All the faithful are caught up in the mystery of grace and have an essential role to exercise in the ministration of the sacraments. They should be so instructed.

Everyone has a role in the salvation of the world in virtue of the unique relationship to Christ Christians possess as a result of baptism. Likewise the sick have such an appointed task in the salvific activity of the Church. In fact, the sick have perhaps an even greater degree of participation in the ongoing salvation of mankind since they are at present fully capable of realizing the paschal mystery of Christ in their own bodies. Their suffering is visible and their pain can be redemptive, not only for themselves but more properly for those who are in need of the saving merits of noble and God-directed suffering. We must once again educate the people that meritorious suffering is a constitutive element in the sacrament of anointing.

It would appear that if the sacrament of the anointing of the sick is to be understood by the people of God, the sick person must be made to recognize the value in his suffering. Since the sick have an active role in the salvation of the world, this unique role is so accomplished by the uniting of his suffering with the sufferings of Christ. In this way the sick follow St. Paul's exhortation that we must make up in our own bodies that which is lacking in the sufferings of Christ. Herein we discover an essential aspect of the ecclesial dimension of sacramentality operative within this particular sacrament.

The sick person's suffering affects the whole people of God. In one manner of speaking, his absence from active participation diminishes the community; yet, in another way, by uniting his pain to that of Christ's, he contributes to the building up of the Mystical Body of Christ through meritorious suffering.

When the sacrament of the anointing of the sick is actually celebrated, still another dimension of ecclesiality is operative — that of authentic worship. Since the sacrament of anointing is an act of worship, and worship implies participation, the sick, through the reception of this sacrament, worship God in a special manner unique to their condition.

The importance of demonstrating to the sick how they contribute to the Church cannot be overemphasized. The sick actually contribute to the general welfare of the Church, if they choose to worship in and through their suffering.

As for what specifically can be done with regard to the liturgical-pastoral renewal of this sacrament, the new rite speaks for itself. So it would seem that the question confronting us is not: "What should be done?" but rather, "How will we carry out this new format for celebration? How will we educate the people for this change?"

Education and catechesis are the key to the renewal of this sacrament. However, one important corollary to all of this might consist in the attempt to bring the community to an awareness of their ministry to the sick and dying. That the entire community of believers has the responsibility of helping and healing their brothers in the Lord must be emphasized. In this way the people of God should come to realize the communal dimension of the sacrament of the anointing of the sick.

Guidelines for the
Anointing of the Sick

• Special care should be taken that those who are dangerously ill (not necessarily unto death) due to sickness, or old age, receive the sacrament of the anointing of the sick as soon as possible.

• It is sufficient for anointing that there be a reasonable and prudent judgment as to the seriousness of the illness. The priest should be the one to make this judgment if the sick person or his family has not as yet requested the anointing.

• The sacrament of anointing may be repeated as often as this becomes necessary. It may be administered during the same illness if in the judgment of the priest the danger of death becomes more serious.

• A sick person ought to be anointed before he or she undergoes surgery whether or not the surgery is the result of dangerous illness (e.g., tonsils, etc.). The reason for this is that in any operation the danger of death is always present to some degree.

• Old persons, even if they are not suffering from a dangerous illness, may be anointed if their age places them in a weakened condition.

• A sick child may be anointed, providing the child has sufficient use of reason to be comforted and uplifted by the sacrament. However, any child who is dangerously ill should always be anointed.

• The unconscious may be anointed if there is reason to presume that had they been conscious they would have requested the sacrament. This also obtains in the case of those who have lost their faculties. This presumption should be broad; the priest therefore should always anoint the unconscious or mentally disabled since he ought always to presume that they would have asked for the sacrament unless he has reason to believe the contrary.

• In the case of those already dead, the priest should pray over the dead person, requesting God to forgive his sins and welcome him into his kingdom. Since the dead are not capable of receiving sacraments, the anointing is not to be administered. However, in doubtful cases those presumed dead may be anointed conditionally.

• In the case where two or more priests are present for the sacrament of anointing, only one of them says the prayer (form of the sacrament) and performs the anointing (matter of the sacrament). Those other priests present may take part in the various parts of the ceremony (readings, invocation, etc.). However, all priests present may, each in his turn, lay hands on the sick person.

• The proper matter for the sacrament of anointing is olive oil, but other plant oil may be substituted if the circumstances suggest and need demands. The oil of the sick (*oleum infirmorum*) is that which is ordinarily blessed by the bishop on Holy Thursday. However, a priest may bless the oil used in this sacrament in time of urgent necessity or when his doing so would benefit the faithful in terms of their comfort and instructions.

• After the rite of anointing, wherein oil blessed by the priest was used, the oil remaining should be absorbed into cotton and burned.

• The sacrament of anointing is conferred by the anointing of the sick person on the forehead and hands. The formula (the words which make up the form of the sacrament) is divided into two parts so that the first part is to be said while the forehead is anointed, with the second part to be said while the hands are anointed.

• However, in most urgent cases (cases of extreme necessity), a single anointing, preferably on the forehead, is sufficient. If it is impossible to anoint the forehead, then any other suitable part of the body is anointed. In either case, the entire formula of the sacrament is to be said.

• Since it is incumbent upon all the baptized, who are able, to receive Holy Viaticum, those in danger of death (broadly interpreted) are obliged to receive the Eucharist. Pastors must ensure that the sacrament is readily available to these persons. This is a grave pastoral obligation.

• When the priest prepares for the celebration of anointing he should take care, except in emergency cases, to ascertain the condition of the sick person and arrange the ceremony accordingly. If possible, the priest should prepare and explain the sacrament in consultation with the sick person's family.

11

Prayers for the Dying

Preparing for death is an experience everyone must face. It is one time the faithful need the helping hand of the priest. Priests gain much joy and satisfaction in being able to give this assistance, in helping people die happily, with full preparation to meet their Creator.

Recommendation of the Departing Soul to God

V. Peace to this house.

R. And to all who live in it.

Let this water (*sprinkling with holy water*) call to mind your baptismal sharing in Christ's redeeming passion and resurrection.

THE LITANY FOR THE DYING

Lord, have mercy.

Christ, have mercy.

Lord, have mercy.

Holy Mary, *pray for him (her).*

[After each invocation, respond with: *Pray for him (her).*]

All you holy angels and archangels,

Holy Abel,

All you choirs of the just,

Holy Abraham,

St. John the Baptist,

St. Joseph,

All you holy patriarchs and prophets,

St. Peter,

St. Paul,

St. Andrew,

St. John,

All you holy apostles and evangelists,

All you holy disciples of the Lord,

All you holy innocents,

St. Stephen,

St. Lawrence,

All you holy martyrs,

St. Sylvester,

St. Gregory,
St. Augustine,
All you holy bishops and confessors,
St. Benedict,
St. Francis,
St. Camillus,
St. John of God,
St. John Neumann,
All you holy monks and hermits,
St. Mary Magdalen,
St. Lucy,
St. Elizabeth Ann Seton,
All you holy virgins and widows,
All you holy saints of God, *intercede for him (her)*.
Be merciful, *spare him (her), O Lord!*
Be merciful, *deliver him (her), O Lord!*
Be merciful, *deliver him (her), O Lord!*

[After each invocation, respond with: *Deliver him (her,) O Lord!*]

From your anger,
From death's dangers,
From an unholy death,
From the punishments of hell,
From every evil,
From the power of the devil,
Through your birth,
Through your cross and passion,
Through your death and burial,
Through your glorious resurrection,
Through your wonderful ascension,
Through the grace of the Holy Spirit, the Consoler,
In the day of judgment,
We who are sinners, *we implore you, hear us.*
That you would spare him (her), *we implore you, hear us.*
Lord, have mercy.
Christ, have mercy.
Lord, have mercy.

PRAYERS

Go forth from this world, O Christian soul, in the name of God the Father almighty, who created you; in the name of Jesus Christ, the Son of the living God, who suffered and died for you; in the name of the Holy Spirit, who sanctified you; in the name of the glorious and holy Mother of God, the Virgin Mary; in the name of blessed Joseph, her illustrious spouse; in the name of the angels, archangels, thrones, dominations, principalities, powers, virtues, cherubim and seraphim; in the name of the patriarchs and prophets; in the name of the holy apostles and evangelists; in the name of the holy martyrs and confessors; in the name of the holy monks and hermits; in the name of the holy virgins and of all the saints of God. May peace come to you today, and may your home be in holy Sion. We ask this through Christ our Lord.

R. Amen.

O God of compassion and kindness, in your boundless mercy you erase the sins of the penitent and remove the guilt of past wrongdoing by the grace of forgiveness. Look with kindness on this your servant, N., and listen to his (her) prayer as he (she) asks with his (her) whole heart for the remission of all his (her) sins. Make new in him (her), O most loving Father, whatever has been damaged by earthly weakness and profaned by the deceit of the devil; and bind to the body of the Church this member who has been redeemed. Listen with mercy to his (her) sighs, O Lord. Look with mercy on his (her) tears; and as his (her) trust is only in your mercy, admit him (her) to the sacrament of reconciliation. We ask this through Christ our Lord.

R. Amen.

Dear brother (sister), I commend you to almighty God, and I entrust you to him who created you, so that, when by your dying you have paid the debt to which every man is subject, you may return to your Maker, to him who formed you from the clay of the earth. Then, when your soul goes forth from your body, may the radiant company of angels come to meet you. May the assembly of the apostles, our judges, welcome you. May the victorious army of white-robed martyrs meet you on your way. May the joyful throng of confessors gather about you. May the glorious choir of virgins receive you. May the patriarchs enfold you in the embrace of blessed peace. May St. Joseph, beloved patron of the dying, fill you with confidence, and may the holy Mother of God, the Virgin Mary, lovingly turn her eyes toward you.

And then, gentle and joyful, may Christ Jesus appear to assign you a place among those who stand forever in his presence. May Christ, who was crucified for your sake, free you from excruciating pain. May Christ, who died for you, free you from the death that never ends. May Christ, the Son of the living God, set you in the ever blooming garden of his paradise, and may he, the true Shepherd, recognize you as one of his own. May he free you from all your sins and assign you a place at his right hand in the company of his elect. May you see your Redeemer face-to-face; and, standing in his presence forever, may you see with joyful eyes Truth revealed in all its fullness. And so, having taken your place in the ranks of the blessed, may you enjoy the happiness of divine contemplation for ever and ever. We ask this through the same Christ our Lord.

R. Amen.

O Lord, receive your servant into the place of salvation which he (she) is hoping to receive from your mercy.

R. Amen.

Deliver your servant, O Lord, from the dangers of hell, from constraining punishments, and from all distress.

R. Amen.

Deliver the soul of your servant, O Lord, as you delivered Noah from the flood.

R. Amen.

Deliver the soul of your servant, O Lord, as you delivered Job from his sufferings.

R. Amen.

Deliver the soul of your servant, O Lord, as you delivered Moses from the power of Pharaoh, king of Egypt.

R. Amen.

Deliver the soul of your servant, O Lord, as you delivered Daniel from the den of lions.

R. Amen.

Deliver the soul of your servant, O Lord, as you delivered the three young men from the fiery furnace and from the power of the unjust king.

R. Amen.

Deliver the soul of your servant, O Lord, as you delivered Susanna from an unjust condemnation.

R. Amen.

Deliver the soul of your servant, O Lord, as you delivered David from the power of King Saul and the might of Goliath.

R. Amen.

Deliver the soul of your servant, O Lord, as you delivered Peter and Paul from prison.

R. Amen.

We commend to you, O Lord, the soul of your servant, N., and we beg of you, O Lord Jesus Christ, Savior of the world, that you would not refuse the welcoming embrace of the patriarchs to this soul for whose sake you in your mercy came down upon earth.

Recognize him (her), O Lord, as your creature, made not by strange gods but by you, the only true and living God, for there is no God other than you, and no works like yours.

Give joy, O Lord, to his (her) soul by the sight of you. Remember not the sins and intemperance he (she) has committed, urged on by the madness and fever of evil desire. Indeed he (she) sinned; yet never did he (she) deny the Father, the Son, and the Holy Spirit, but believed in them, had zeal for God's cause, and faithfully adored him who made all things. We ask this through Christ our Lord.

R. Amen.

We implore you, O Lord, do not remember the faults of his (her) youth and his (her) ignorance; but rather through your great mercy, be mindful of him (her) in the splendor of your glory. May heaven open for him (her); may the angels rejoice with him (her). Receive your servant, O Lord, into your kingdom. May he (she) be taken up by holy Michael, the archangel of God, who leads the armies of heaven. May the holy angels of God come to meet him (her) and take him (her) into the heavenly Jerusalem. May he (she) be welcomed by blessed Peter, the apostle to whom God gave the keys of the kingdom of heaven. May he (she) be aided by St. Paul, the apostle who was worthy to be God's chosen instrument. May St. John, the favored apostle of God to whom were revealed the secrets of heaven, intercede for him (her). May all the holy apostles, on whom has been conferred the power of binding and loosing, pray for him (her). May all who have endured great sufferings in this world for the sake of Christ, the saints and the chosen of God, intercede for him (her), so that, freed from the bonds of the flesh, he (she) may attain to the glory of the kingdom of heaven. Through the help of our Lord Jesus Christ, who with the Father and the Holy Spirit, lives and reigns for ever and ever.

R. Amen.

O Virgin most kind, Mary, Mother of God, most loving consoler of those in distress, commend to your Son the soul of his servant, N., so that, because of your motherly intervention, he (she) may be freed from the terrors of death, and may joyfully arrive, in your company, at his (her) longed-for home in heaven. We ask this through Christ our Lord.

R. Amen.

To you do I turn for refuge, St. Joseph, patron of the dying, at whose happy deathbed Jesus and Mary stood watch. Because of this twofold pledge of hope, I earnestly commend to you the soul of this servant, N., in his (her) last agony; so that he (she) may, with you as protector, be set free from the snares of the devil and from everlasting death, and may attain to everlasting joy. We ask this through Christ our Lord.

R. Amen.

PRAYERS AT THE TIME OF DEATH

Into your hands, O Lord, I commend my spirit!
Lord Jesus Christ, receive my spirit.

Holy Mary, pray for me.

Mary, Mother of grace, Mother of mercy, protect me from the enemy, and receive me at the hour of my death.

St. Joseph, pray for me.

St. Joseph, with your spouse, the Blessed Virgin, open to me the heart of divine mercy!

Jesus, Mary and Joseph, I give you my heart and my soul!

Jesus, Mary and Joseph, assist me in my last agony!

Jesus, Mary and Joseph, in your blessed company may I sleep and rest in peace.

R. Come to his (her) aid, O saints of God; come forth to meet him (her), angels of the Lord, receiving his (her) soul, presenting it to the Most High.

V. May Christ, who has called you, now receive you, and may the angels bring you to Abraham's bosom.

R. Receiving his (her) soul, presenting it to the Most High.

V. Eternal rest grant unto him (her), O Lord, and let perpetual light shine upon him (her).

R. Receiving his (her) soul, presenting it to the Most High.

Lord, have mercy.

Christ, have mercy.

Lord, have mercy.

Our Father . . .

V. And lead us not into temptation.

R. But deliver us from evil.

V. Eternal rest grant unto him (her), O Lord.

R. And let perpetual light shine upon him (her).

V. From the gates of hell.

R. Save his (her) soul, O Lord.

V. May he (she) rest in peace.

R. Amen.

V. O Lord, hear my prayer.

R. And let my cry come to you.

V. The Lord be with you.

R. And also with you.

Let us pray.

O Lord, we commend to you the soul of your servant, N., that, having departed from this world, he (she) may live with you. By the grace of your merciful love wash away the sins that in human frailty he (she) has committed in this life. We ask this through Christ our Lord.

R. Amen.

Grant, O Lord, that, while we here lament the departure of your servant, we may ever remember that we are most certainly to follow him (her). Give us grace to prepare for that last hour by a good life, that we may not be surprised by a sudden death, but be ever watching when you will call, so that we may enter into eternal glory. We ask this through Christ our Lord.

R. Amen.

12

Wake Services

This scriptural service does not require the people to have any cards, booklets or similar aids. Due to the nature and practical structuring of a service of consolation, it is preferable that the passing out of booklets, etc., not be done, simply because it is not necessary. To do so adds frequently to the already existing mental confusion of the bereaved.

Furthermore, the recitation of the rosary ought not to be summarily dismissed as an outdated and meaningless prayer form. Clearly, our Lady's prayer is anything but meaningless. Rather, the minister should take pains to place, before the family, the option of either a scriptural service or the rosary. This should be done evenhandedly. That is to say, not emphasizing the scriptural service and downplaying the rosary simply because the minister does not approve of the rosary. The operating principle must always be, "Let the family decide."

Do not multiply prayer services. It stands to reason that if the Knights of Columbus, the Veterans of Foreign Wars, the American Legion, the Rosary Society, etc., plan to conduct a service of prayer for their deceased member, the priest or deacon should not insist on following up with his own service. Perhaps in the event that one or other of these groups or societies conduct their service, the minister should then either come to the wake on another night to celebrate the service of consolation, or, if the minister is scheduled for the same night, then he might request to say a simple prayer, a few words of consolation and faith (one or two minutes) and a blessing.

A Celebration of Consolation: The Wake Service

GREETING **In the name of the Father, and of the Son, and of the Holy Spirit.**

MINISTER *A Reading From the Second Letter of Paul to the Corinthians (1:3-4)*

Praised be God, the Father of our Lord Jesus Christ, the Father of mercies,

and the God of all consolation! He comforts us in all our afflictions and thus enables us to comfort those who are in trouble, with the same consolation we have received from him.

BRIEF WORD OF INTRODUCTION AND CONSOLATION For example: "Why are we gathered here in prayer? What should be our hope? From whom will we gather our strength to meet the difficult days which lie ahead?"
This should be personal, addressed to those present. By all means it should not be read or recited.

SILENT BLESSING
OF THE BODY

PRAYERFUL RECITATION OF A PSALM   See the Appendix at the end of this chapter for alternate psalms.

PSALM 116   The response is taken from Psalm 62:8.

R. Unburden your hearts to him, God is a shelter for us.

V. I love! For Yahweh listens
    to my entreaty;
he bends down to listen to me
    when I call.

R. Unburden your hearts to him, God is a shelter for us.

V. Death's cords were tightening 'round me,
    the nooses of Sheol;
distress and anguish gripped me,
    I invoked the name of Yahweh:
"Yahweh, rescue me!"

R. Unburden your hearts to him, God is a shelter for us.

V. Yahweh is righteous and merciful,
    our God is tenderhearted;

Yahweh defends the simple,
>   he saved me when I was brought to
>   my knees.

R.   Unburden your hearts to him, God is a
>   shelter for us.

V.   Return to your resting place, my soul,
>   Yahweh has treated you kindly.
>   He has rescued (me from death) my
>   eyes from tears
>   and my feet from stumbling. . . .

R.   Unburden your hearts to him, God is a
>   shelter for us.

V.   The death of the devout
>   costs Yahweh dear . . .
>   [I have faith, even when I say,
>   "I am completely crushed"].

R.   Unburden your hearts to him, God is a
>   shelter for us.

V.   I will offer you the thanksgiving sacri-
>   fice,
>   invoking the name of Yahweh.
>   I will walk in Yahweh's presence
>   in the land of the living.

R.   Unburden your hearts to him, God is a
>   shelter for us.

PRAYER   O almighty Father, we seek the
shelter of your wings like young birds
flocking to their mother's side. Pour
your consoling grace upon all of us
gathered here before you, that we
might unburden our heavy hearts. We
ask you to look kindly upon your departed servant, N.; welcome him
(her) into the company of your saints,
where tears are no more. Hear gra-

ciously our prayer of faith we address to you in the name of your Son, our Lord Jesus Christ, who lives and rules with you and the Holy Spirit, one God for ever and ever. Amen.

SCRIPTURE
READING

Select either of the two readings from the New Testament [below], or consult the Appendix at the end of this chapter for alternate texts.

The minister speaks a few brief words of consolation based on God's word, or more directly on the bidding prayer.

MINISTER

A Reading From the Letter of Paul to the Philippians (3:17, 19-21)

Be imitators of me, my brothers. Take as your guide those who follow the example that we set. . . . Such as these will end in disaster! Their god is their belly and their glory is in their shame. I am talking about those who are set upon the things of this world. As you well know, we have our citizenship in heaven; it is from there that we eagerly await the coming of our Savior, the Lord Jesus Christ. He will give a new form to this lowly body of ours and remake it according to the pattern of his glorified body, by his power to subject everything to himself.

This is the word of the Lord.

Or:

A Reading From the Gospel According to Luke (24:1-8)

On the first day of the week, at dawn, the women came to the tomb bringing the spices they had prepared. They found the stone rolled back from the

162

tomb; but when they entered the tomb, they did not find the body of the Lord Jesus. While they were still at a loss over what to think of this, two men in dazzling garments stood beside them. The men said to them: "Why do you search for the Living One among the dead? He is not here; he has been raised up. Remember what he said to you while he was still in Galilee — that the Son of Man must be delivered into the hands of sinful men, and be crucified, and on the third day rise again?" With this reminder, his words came back to them.

This is the gospel of the Lord.

THE BIDDING
PRAYER
(GENERAL
INTERCESSION)

R. Lord, unburden the hearts of your people.

V. For N., that his (her) heart and soul might find a peaceful dwelling in the bosom of God and the fellowship of the saints, we pray to the Lord.

R. Lord, unburden the hearts of your people.

V. For all here present, grieving as we are at the loss of our dear brother (sister), that God might wipe away our tears and grant us the consolation of his grace, we pray to the Lord.

R. Lord, unburden the hearts of your people.

V. For all those who have recently lost a loved one, that God might see them

163

through their human sorrow and grant them the consoling vision of his kingdom, we pray to the Lord.

R. Lord, unburden the hearts of your people.

V. Finally, for all those who have gone before us marked with the sign of faith, that they, seated as they are around the table of the Lord, might prayerfully assert us who remain, we pray to the Lord.

R. Lord, unburden the hearts of your people.

CLOSING PRAYER O God our consoling Father, we have gathered here in prayer to invoke your goodness upon our departed loved one, N., and seek for ourselves your strength to carry on. We pray you dry our tears with your words of faith and let us behold the vision of your eternal banquet table where one day, united again with our beloved N., we might praise you for ever and ever. Amen.

ALL The Lord's Prayer is said by the assembly.

BLESSING

Appendix of Scriptural Texts for Wake Service

ALTERNATE SCRIPTURAL TEXTS *A Reading From the Letter of Paul to the Romans (14:7-10)* The life and death of each of us has its influence on others; if we live, we live for the Lord; and if we die, we die for the Lord, so that alive or dead we belong to the Lord. This explains why Christ both died and came to life: it was so that he might be Lord both of the dead and of the living.

A Reading From the First Letter of Paul to the Corinthians (15:51-57)

I will tell you something that has been secret: that we are not all going to die, but we shall all be changed. This will be instantaneous, in the twinkling of an eye, when the last trumpet sounds. It will sound, and the dead will be raised, imperishable, and we shall be changed as well, because our present perishable nature must put on imperishability and this mortal nature must put on immortality. When this perishable nature has put on imperishability, and when this mortal nature has put on immortality, then the words of Scripture will come true: Death is swallowed up in victory. Death, where is your victory? Death, where is your sting?

A Reading From the First Letter of Paul to the Thessalonians (4:13-15)

We want to be quite certain, brothers, about those who have died, to make sure that you do not grieve about them, like the other people who have no hope. We believe that Jesus died and rose again, and that it will be the same for those who have died in Jesus: God will bring them with him.

165

A Reading From the Second Letter of Paul to Timothy (2:11-13)
Here is a saying that you can rely on:
If we have died with him, then we shall
    live with him.
If we hold firm, then we shall reign
    with him.
If we disown him, then he will disown
    us.
We may be unfaithful, but he is always
    faithful,
for he cannot disown his own self.

A Reading From the Book of Revelation (14:13)
Then I heard a voice from heaven say to me, "Write down: Happy are those who die in the Lord! Happy indeed, the Spirit says; now they can rest forever after their work, since their good deeds go with them."

ALTERNATE
PSALM TEXTS

PSALM 23

R. The Lord is my shepherd; I shall not
    want.

V. The Lord is my shepherd; I shall not
    want.
    In verdant pastures he gives me
      repose;
  Beside restful waters he leads me;
    he refreshes my soul.

R. The Lord is my shepherd; I shall not
    want.

V. He guides me in right paths
    for his name's sake.

Even though I walk in the dark valley
    I fear no evil; for you are at my
      side
With your rod and your staff
    that give me courage.

R. The Lord is my shepherd; I shall not
      want.

V. You spread the table before me
    in the sight of my foes;
You anoint my head with oil;
    my cup overflows.

R. The Lord is my shepherd; I shall not
      want.

V. Only goodness and kindness follow me
    all the days of my life;
And I shall dwell in the house of the
    Lord
    for years to come.

R. The Lord is my shepherd; I shall not
      want.

PSALM 130

R. Out of the depths I cry to you, O Lord.

V. Out of the depths I cry to you, O Lord;
    Lord, hear my voice!
Let your ears be attentive
    to my voice in supplication:

R. Out of the depths I cry to you, O Lord.

V. If you, O Lord, mark iniquities,
    Lord, who can stand?
But with you is forgiveness,
    that you may be revered.

R. Out of the depths I cry to you, O Lord.

V. I trust in the Lord;
    my soul trusts in his word.

My soul waits for the Lord
  more than sentinels wait for the
  dawn.

R. Out of the depths I cry to you, O Lord.

V. More than sentinels wait for the dawn,
  let Israel wait for the Lord,
For with the Lord is kindness
  and with him is plenteous redemption;
And he will redeem Israel
  from all their iniquities.

R. Out of the depths I cry to you, O Lord.

PSALM 62

R. Only in God is my soul at rest.

V. Only in God is my soul at rest;
  from him comes my salvation.
He only is my rock and my salvation,
  my stronghold; I shall not be dis-
  turbed at all. . . .

R. Only in God is my soul at rest.

V. Only in God be at rest, my soul,
  for from him comes my hope.
He only is my rock and my salvation,
  my stronghold; I shall not be dis-
  turbed. . . .

R. Only in God is my soul at rest.

V. Trust in him at all times, O my people!
  Pour out your hearts before him;
  God is our refuge!. . .

R. Only in God is my soul at rest.

ADDITIONAL
SCRIPTURAL
TEXTS

*A Reading From the Holy Gospel
According to Luke (7:11-17)*
Soon afterward he went to a town
called Naim, and his disciples and a

large crowd accompanied him. As he approached the gate of the town a dead man was being carried out, the only son of a widowed mother. A considerable crowd of townsfolk were with her. The Lord was moved with pity upon seeing her and said to her, "Do not cry." Then he stepped forward and touched the litter; at this, the bearers halted. He said, "Young man, I bid you get up." The dead man sat up and began to speak. Then Jesus gave him back to his mother. Fear seized them all and they began to praise God. "A great prophet has risen among us," they said; and, "God has visited his people." This was the report that spread about him throughout Judea and the surrounding country.

A Reading From the Holy Gospel According to John (11:21-27)
Martha said to Jesus: "Lord, if you had been here, my brother would never have died. Even now, I am sure that God will give you whatever you ask of him." "Your brother will rise again," Jesus assured her. "I know he will rise again," Martha replied, "in the resurrection on the last day." Jesus told her:
"I am the resurrection and the life: whoever believes in me,
though he should die, will come to life; and whoever is alive and believes in
        me
will never die.
Do you believe this?" "Yes, Lord," she replied. "I have come to believe that you are the Messiah, the Son of

God: he who is to come into the
world."

*A Reading From the Holy Gospel
According to John (14:1-4)*
"Do not let your hearts be troubled.
Have faith in God
and faith in me.
In my Father's house there are many
dwelling places;
otherwise, how could I have told you
that I was going to prepare a place for
you?
I am indeed going to prepare a place
for you,
and then I shall come back to take you
with me,
that where I am you also may be.
You know the way that leads where I
go."

13

Christian Burial

(With Appropriate Homilies)

Vigil Service on the Eve of Burial

EXHORTATION Beloved in the Lord:
Or:

My dearest friends:
Or:

My brothers and sisters:
Or:

My fellow believers in the Lord:
Or some other similar expression of greeting.

St. Paul has exhorted us who have been given the great hope of everlasting life through the blood of Jesus (cf. Hebrews 10:19) not to sorrow as those who have no hope. For we believe that Jesus died and rose again, and that he will also bring with him to his Father those who sleep in him. Let us therefore hold fast the confession of our hope without wavering, for he who promised is faithful.

We are burdened with sadness at the departure of our brother (sister), N.; but we know that for those who have put their trust in the Lord Jesus, our separation is only for a time. While we remember our brother's (sister's) life with us, and of God's goodness to him (her), let us also consider on this night how to stir up one another to greater love and good works (cf. Hebrews

10:24). For God is love, and he who abides in love, abides in God, and God in him (cf. 1 John 4:16).

PRAYER Let us pray.

Heavenly Father, we pray that you will keep in tender love the life of your beloved servant, N. We shall always remember him (her), and your goodness in allowing us to share our lives here on earth. Help us who remain here to serve you steadfastly, with a sure trust in your promise of eternal life. For we could live now for that day when we will be united with our brother (sister), and all your blessed children, in everlasting glory, through Jesus Christ our Lord. Amen.

READINGS* *A Reading From the Letter of Paul to the Romans (8:31-39)*

What shall we say after that? If God is for us, who can be against us? Is it possible that he who did not spare his own Son but handed him over for the sake of us all will not grant us all things besides? Who shall bring a charge against God's chosen ones? God, who justifies? Who shall condemn them? Christ Jesus, who died or rather was raised up, who is at the right hand of God and who intercedes for us?

Who will separate us from the love of Christ? Trial, or distress, or persecution, or hunger, or nakedness, or danger, or the sword? As Scripture says: "For your sake we are being

*Other suggested readings include: 1 Corinthians 13; 1 Corinthians 15:51-58; Ephesians 2:1-10; Hebrews 11 and 12:2.

172

slain all the day long; we are looked upon as sheep to be slaughtered." Yet in all this we are more than conquerors because of him who has loved us. For I am certain that neither death nor life, neither angels nor principalities, neither the present nor the future, nor powers, neither height nor depth nor any other creature, will be able to separate us from the love of God that comes to us in Christ Jesus our Lord.

HOMILY   Brief words of consolation of a personal nature.

NUNC DIMITTIS   Recited antiphonally.

V. Lord, now let your servant depart in peace.

R. According to your word.

V. For my eyes have seen your salvation.

R. Which you have prepared in the sight of all peoples.

V. A light to enlighten the Gentiles.

R. And the glory of your people Israel.

V. Glory be to the Father, and to the Son, and to the Holy Spirit.

R. As it was in the beginning, is now and ever shall be, world without end. Amen.

V. The Lord be with you.

R. And also with you.

PRAYER   Let us pray.
Heavenly Father, we ask you to look in tender pity and compassion upon your beloved servants here present, whose joy has been turned into sadness. Send

them your peace and comfort. Help them to be drawn closer to you and to one another by their shared sorrow. Strengthen and preserve them in true faith, that they may hold fast to your promise of a day wherein all mysteries shall be revealed, and all tears shall be wiped away. And for these mercies, we shall praise your name, through Jesus Christ our Lord. Amen.

FINAL BLESSING   May the Lord bless you and keep you.
May the Lord make his face shine upon you and be gracious to you.
May the Lord lift up his countenance upon you and give you peace. Amen.

Funeral Mass

CHURCH

Preparations
• Usual vestments (white, purple, black) for celebrant and for concelebrants, if any.
• Lectionary and Sacramentary.
• Holy water and incense.
• White pall for coffin.
• Paschal candle or lighted candles to be placed around the coffin.

CEMETERY

Preparations
• Holy water and incense.
• Sacramentary.
• Violet stole.

Rite at the Entrance of the Church

GREETING   The priest, accompanied by the ministers, may begin the rite at the door of the church,

FOR WAKES OR OTHER FUNERAL SERVICES

IT HAS BEEN THE CUSTOM FOR CENTURIES FOR PEOPLE TO
GATHER TOGETHER TO PAY TRIBUTE TO THE DEAD.

THE CHRISTIANS WERE NO EXCEPTION. FROM THE EARLIEST
DAYS OF THE CHURCH, THE COMMUNITY GATHERED TO PAY ITS
RESPECTS TO A FELLOW CHRISTIAN WHO, BY BAPTISM, HAD
BECOME A REPRESENTATIVE OF CHRIST IN THIS WORLD.

TONIGHT(TODAY) WE ASSEMBLE (ON THE EVENING BEFORE
THE BURIAL) TO PAY OUR RESPECTS TO...... AND SHARE
WITH ONE ANOTHER THE HOPE AND CONSOLATION OF OUR FAITH.

THIS TRIBUTE, THIS HARING OF OUR COMMON HOPE, IS
CALLED "THE CHRISTIAN WAKE SERVICE."

WE INVITE YOU ALL TO TAKE PART IN THIS RITUAL AND
TO RECITE OUT ALOUD THE PRAYERS AND THE PSALMS FROM
THE BOOKLET.

START WITH: ALMIGHTY FATHER, WHEN ONE OF OUR LOVED ONES
DIES, OUR FAITH AND TRUST IN YOU ARE PUT TO TEST. WE
DRAW TOGETHER IN THE PAIN OF THIS LOSS; TURN OUR ANXIETY IN
INTO CONFIDENCE AND OUR SORROW INTO JOY, BECAUSE YOUR
SON HAS CONQUERED DEATH. WE ASK YOU ALSO, FATHER, TO
REVIVE YOUR SERVANT... AND FULFILL YOUR PROMISES TO
HIM (HER). HE(SHE) LOVED YOU IN LIFE: DO NOT FORSAKE HIM
(HER) IN DEATH. WE ASK YOU THIS THROUGH CHRIST,OUR LORD.

II OTHER PRAYERS

LET US PRAY: O GOD, THE LORD OF ALL CREATION WHO HAS THE POWER OF LIFE AND DEATH, WHO CAN BESTOW LIFE UPON HUMANKIND AND CALL THEM TO DEATH, YOU WELCOME THE SOULS OF YOUR HOLY ONES, AND BRING THEM TO ETERNAL LIFE: BUT YOU ALONE ARE INCURRUPTIBLE, UNCHANGING, ETERNAL. WE BEG YOU, BRING YOUR SERVANT...TO SHARE IN YOUR KINGDOM ACCORDING TO   HIS   HER MERITS.THROUGH YOUR HOLY SPIRIT SOOTHE THE GRIEF OF THOSE WHO SURVIVE   HIM   HER MERCIFULLY PURIFY THE SOUL OF YOUR SERVANT...FROM EVERY STAIN OF SIN, SO THAT   HE   SHE MAY QUICKLY BE ADMITTED TO THE JOY OF YOUR BEATIFIC VISION, TO THE JOY OF YOUR ETERNAL LOVE, THROUGH CHRIST OUR LORD, . AMEN.

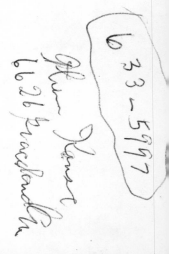

using one of the apostolic greetings of the Mass.

PRIEST **The grace of our Lord Jesus Christ and the love of God and the fellowship of the Holy Spirit be with you all.**

RESPONSE **And also with you.**

Or:

PRIEST **The grace and peace of our Father and the Lord Jesus Christ be with you.**

RESPONSE **Blessed be God, the Father of our Lord Jesus Christ.**
(*Or:* And also with you.)

The priest may then sprinkle the body with holy water saying these or similar words:

PRIEST **I bless the body of N., with the holy water that recalls (his) her baptism of which St. Paul writes: All of us who were baptized into Christ Jesus were baptized into his death. By baptism into his death we were buried together with him, so that just as Christ was raised from the dead by the glory of the Father, we too might live a new life.**
For if we have been united with him by likeness to his death, so shall we be united with him by likeness to his resurrection.

A white pall, in remembrance of the baptismal garment, may then be placed on the coffin by the pallbearers or others, and the priest may say these or similar words:

On the day of his (her) baptism, N. put on Christ. In the day of Christ's coming, may he (she) be clothed with glory.

General Funeral Homily 1

The Bible has endured to a large measure because it has assisted mankind in dealing with and handling the unwelcome and the tragic events in life. In the New Testament the early Christians knew well the anxiety and tears that faith is called upon to bear, sooner or later. Those early believers needed strength, as we all do from time to time, in order to handle the grim reality that life has a sorrowful dimension.

To help the early Christians in the city of Corinth, St. Paul addressed these words to them: "Blessed be the God and Father of our Lord Jesus Christ, the Father of mercies and the God of all comfort, who comforts us in all our afflictions, so that we may be able to comfort those who are in any affliction with the same comfort we ourselves have received from God."

Paul knew full well that those who were suffering needed others to lighten their burden; that they especially needed to know that God was with them, not unfeelingly but intimately sharing in their sorrow and tears. Paul gives us a clue to the reality and power of faith. For Paul faith is bold in its dealing with death. That faith provides the strength to look death straight in the eye while saying, "We shall overcome; blessed be God forever."

Our time has arrived to experience the stinging pain of death. We feel no joy at this moment in our lives. Rather we experience an emptiness of unbounded proportion and a loss too profound for words to express. You feel, deep within your heart, a pain known but to God. He is with us today, in a most special way to help us bear our own cross.

That Christ shed tears is recorded only twice in the

gospel writings. One was over the death of a city, Jerusalem, and the other over the death of a friend, Lazarus. By shedding tears himself, Jesus sanctified the tears we shed over the loss of our loved one. You see, Jesus understands. God knows we must cry, for we are in pain. Yet he tells us that while we weep and mourn for a time, our sorrow will somehow turn into joy by faith. When all is said and done, faith is all we have left.

We turn our eyes now toward God, the Father of mercy and the God of all consolation. Nothing is more crucial for us in this time of sorrow than the view we have of God. Our God is a God of mercy, a master of sympathy, a Father of loving comfort. His gentle hand rests upon our shoulder as we feebly shoulder our heartbreaking grief. God is with us, sharing in grace and promising that we shall meet our beloved again in resurrection. He supports us with loyal friends and the faith he so generously provides. He proclaims that the Church in heaven and the Church on earth are one. That, truly, we are not separated in love from our beloved. One day soon we will all share the same table once more. He assures us of an eternal homecoming where even tears will be wiped away and the love and presence of our deceased, a presence we seem to have lost, will be regained forever.

Every day, but especially today, let us rejoice in the truth that we are surrounded by a "great cloud of witnesses" and that N. is a part of that company of saints.

The Father of our Lord Jesus Christ,
The Father of mercies,
The God of all consolation —
May he keep you in his peace.

General Funeral Homily 2

Life is a mystery — life is full of mysteries when we really stop to analyze it. Frequently when things happen that upset and disturb us, we never ask the "how" of the situation but rather the "why"; and the lack of a solution to our questioning makes it that much more mysterious. The problems of life — sickness, hardships, trials of one kind or another, disappointments, heartaches, troubles of various descriptions, many times very difficult to accept — these are all so mysterious to us. But the problems of life being a mystery become more difficult at the time of death. Again we are inclined to ask: "Why?" And yet death is the one thing in life of which you and I are certain. We all know that we must die; we know that death comes sometimes when least expected, that it comes to our loved ones; and we know that we must all face it ourselves.

I am reminded of what an anonymous author wrote, and I quote:

"Friends come, friends go; the loves men know are ever fleeting. With warmth and cheer they linger near, the friends we fondly treasure; then on a day they drift away, a loss no words can measure.

"And though we grieve to see them leave, in thought we still enfold them. They come, they go, these loves we know. Life's tides are ever moving. But year on year, they still seem near, so great the power of loving."

N., a strong and sterling person, loved life as is evidenced by the complete dedication he (she) gave to it; and by love I mean not merely affection but, above all, sharing with others their joys, their sorrows, their heartaches, their blessings. He (she) loved his (her) religion; he (she) loved his (her) God and served him well by instilling into his (her) family the ideals of genuine Christian love. The Scripture text, "Love one another as I have loved you," was a very real thing for him (her), a dynamic conviction and a heritage he (she) has so nobly bequeathed to his (her) family and his (her) many friends.

I think too that N., a quiet unassuming person, whom today we commend to his (her) Creator, disliked eulogies. And why? Perhaps he (she) felt like Cardinal John Heenan, the late archbishop of Westminster, who remarked that when he died he wanted no panegyric for fear people would deprive him of the prayers he really needed from his friends.

An epitaph* inscribed on N.'s grave could appropriately read: "No truly good person dies. Like a star which has become extinct but whose light lingers on for generations to gladden the eyes of man, so too this person will linger on as a light in our memories." May the good God be merciful to his (her) soul!

Homily for Funerals 1

(This homily has as its basis John 14:1-6 and 1 Corinthians 15:51-57, but may be used with other funeral texts.)

At times like these we are full of questions. We want to know "why." Why this mystery of death? Why here and now? Why so close to home?

Being so full of questions, we are like the doubting Thomas of the gospel, and there's nothing wrong with a few puzzling doubts. But one question after another only leads to more questions. Jesus understands our questions as he understood Thomas's. The answer he gave Thomas, he gives to us: "Don't let your hearts be troubled." Don't worry, calm down and don't be upset. "Have faith in God and faith in me. . . . I am preparing a place for you."

We do have faith, but that doesn't take away our questions. We want to know where this "place" is and how to get there. And why is it that we must experience this mystery of death in order to get to the "place" Jesus has pre-

---

*Suggested alternate epitaphs include:

• "The love and esteem of all who knew him (her) is the best testimony of his (her) real character" *(Salisbury Cathedral, England)*.

• "He (she) lived beloved, and died lamented" *(Chester Cathedral, England)*.

• "A gentleman in whom the various social, domestic and religious virtues were eminently united. The uniform rectitude of his conduct commended the esteem of others, while the benevolence of his manners secured their love."

• "What a holy, good man, almost beyond description! Not defeated by hard work, not to be defeated by death, he neither feared to die nor refused to live."

pared for us? St. Paul helps to answer our questions too. He says that in this mystery of death, we shall be changed, in a moment, in the twinkling of an eye. We shall all be changed — for the better. We know that what is of the flesh and physical is not permanent. Our bodies are fragile; we have to handle them with care. They break easily.

Our bodies are susceptible to sickness and disease. And even if we are very careful and fortunate enough never to suffer a serious accident or disease, our fragile bodies cannot escape the clock of time. In fact, part of our nature is like a clock that runs for a good long while, but when we begin to age and grow old, the clock runs down. Finally, the time runs out and the clock stops ticking; it simply stops.

That part of our nature which is fragile and running out dies at death. But death is not the end of the story. Death is not an end but a change. Everything about us which is weak and breakable is changed at death into what is strong, unbreakable, healthy and full of vitality. Death is the change for the better. A change from what can die into what lives on and on, never running out. This is eternal life. Death is that doorway into fuller, complete and everlasting life.

Still, we have questions like the doubting Thomas. We want to know "why." Why death here at this time? Why this mystery of death so close to home? The answer is so that the mystery of *life* can be here now, so close to home.

Homily for Funerals 2

(This homily has as its basis John 11:21-27, but may be used with other funeral texts.)

Belief in a person is always easier than belief in a thing or cause. We would be reluctant to put our life at stake without some personal attachment to an individual associated with what it is we believe in.

For instance, many of our forefathers wanted freedom and liberty; but how many would have fought for it if they did not believe in George Washington? Personal belief in his individual leadership and military skill made the risk to life and limb easier to accept.

In our original burst of enthusiasm, we may support and encourage a cause or even an impersonal group of people, like a team. But unless we can identify with an individual person connected with the team, our enthusiasm wanes and we lose interest, not to mention belief. Let a person like Vince Lombardi or Woody Hayes be the leader of the group, then many would passionately follow and believe in that person even when the chips are down.

Belief in a *person*, a real individual, is easier than just believing in a cause or an ideology. We can identify with a real person. Belief in a concept or abstract formulation is much more difficult. And when the situation is trying, or hard to understand, or we're on the losing side, we need faith in a person to keep us going. Right now we need faith in the person of Jesus. Jesus did not require his followers to put their faith in abstract doctrines or promises. He simply said: "Believe in me." When Martha's brother Lazarus died, Jesus did not ask her to believe in the "doctrine" of the resurrection. He asked her to put her faith in him; in the God-man, the real, live person of Jesus Christ.

This is much easier because of all the personal qualities that a doctrine doesn't have, but a person does have. Jesus knows us, he understands us. He sympathized with Martha over the death of her brother whom he loved as a close friend. He sympathizes with us over this death. More than that, he asks us to believe in *him*. He asked Martha if she believed her brother would rise again. She gave a rather matter-of-fact "Yes." But when Jesus said, "I am the resurrection and the life," how different her faith in the resurrection became.

We can believe in the resurrection because we believe in the person of Jesus. It's easy because Jesus himself experienced what we are going through right now. Jesus experienced as a person what the one who has died experienced. Jesus experienced suffering and death for *us*, because he loves us. That's real personal attachment and understanding.

Jesus says to us, as he said to the grieving Martha, "I am the resurrection and the life. Anyone who believes in *me* shall never die."

Do you believe this? We answer: "Yes, Lord! For you are the Messiah, the Son of God."

Funeral Homily for a Public Servant

Jesus once said, "He who believes in me, who clings to me, who keeps my word, who embraces my cross, shall never die." He asked his followers if they believed him, and they responded, "Lord, to whom shall we go? You have the words of eternal life." Jesus himself said, "I am the way, the truth and the life." All of the theologians who study and write in order to explain for us what a life committed in faith to Christ's word means, all the Scripture scholars who lay bare for us the treasures of the Holy Bible, all of the bishops, together with the Pope, whose pastoral exhortations lead us in the way of righteousness—all of these could never speak to us as eloquently and as convincingly as this good man's (woman's) life of faith that we lovingly recall this morning.

He (she) was invited by his (her) Master to climb with him to Calvary, and he (she) responded in faith: "Lord, I will drink your chalice." And so it was, like gold refined in a furnace, that he (she) accepted completely the task set before him (her), the pain and anguish which attends to the way of righteousness. He (she) accepted whatever personal sufferings came his (her) way. He (she) always bowed his (her) head to our heavenly Father's awesome majesty, and said in simple faith, "Your will be done."

Again and again he (she) refused the acclaim offered him (her) by men if only he (she) would compromise what he (she) knew in his (her) conscience was the commanding word of Jesus. As he (she) anguished over what appeared to him (her) to be prestige and comfort gained by others at the expense of Christian principle, he (she) nevertheless steadfastly declined to betray the word of God dwelling in him (her). He (she) never compromised the word of God. It always took the highest priority in every aspect of his (her) human life, and by his (her) faith, which so permeated his (her) total being, he (she) sought instead to lift men up to embrace the same divine vision to which he (she) was committed by his (her) baptism in the Lord Jesus. For he (she) knew that "unless the Lord builds the house, its builder labors in vain." His (her) years of public service to his (her) fellowmen stand for all to see without the slightest taint or blemish.

The Lord truly reigned in his faithful servant, as he promised: "Anyone who loves me will observe my teaching, and my Father will love him, and we will come to him and live with him." Through his (her) embrace of the cross, the glory of resurrection joy was foretasted. Blessed with a wife (husband) in whom God's sacred word dwells with equal intensity, they together built a marriage resplendent with the vision of St. Paul's sublime teaching. Let him who today would inquire or seek to understand what we Catholics believe about marriage in the Lord, run not to a catechism but first hasten to gaze at these two Christian lives. Let him who would doubt the power of the gospel to bring true happiness, peace and joy to the world, witness it in the lives of his wife (her husband) and children who were confirmed and strengthened by our deceased brother's (sister's) lifelong example. This is why we wear white vestments today. This is why the Church triumphant rejoices with the Church militant today. This is the victory that we celebrate today, the faith that overcomes the world.

Well done, [*full name*]! You have enriched your family and friends; you have served your community in total integrity; you have brought honor and credibility to the Church of Jesus Christ. Well done, good and faithful servant, true friend!

Long after our poor and inadequate words will have faded from human memory, long after our hymns of praise and alleluias will have echoed from this house of God, long after our merciful Savior will have dried our tear-filled eyes with his gentle grace, even then will souls yet unknown and still untouched feel the influence of your magnificent faith. Even then will you hear that glorious summons to which we all aspire, even as if for the first time: "Come, blessed of my Father. Receive the kingdom prepared for you from the foundation of the world. Come! Share the joy of your Lord!"

Funeral Homily for a Child

It was once said that the old must die, the young may. There is perhaps no deeper sorrow than that of losing a child. Not only because the little one might be of our own flesh and blood, but more properly because he or she never had the chance to engage in meaningful living. The young are so alive that seeing them dead brings home to all of us the stark reality of the passing of life.

Yet we are alive with hope even if we lack joy today, for we know from the Scriptures that God looked kindly and favorably upon children. Jesus was frequently in the habit of holding a child upon his knee and using the innocence and simplicity of a child to teach a profound biblical message. It is for this reason that we look to the future with hope. Not that God is cruel, but that he reserves a special place in his kingdom for the little child.

Recall how Mary always shows herself in apparitions to children at Lourdes, Fatima, La Salette, etc. Not only does Jesus view children with unique concern and love, but so too does his wonderful mother, who herself knew the pain of losing her Child. When Mary arrived at the sealed tomb she found that even her Son's body could not be viewed or touched. Deprived of the physical presence of her Son Jesus, she was even now denied his lifeless body. Mary felt alone. Surely Mary must have felt then what we all are feeling today as our loved one returns to the earth from whence he or she comes.

The inevitable moment occurs for all of us when in sorrow and tears we face that pain of aloneness only death can bring. Even our Lady was not spared this terrible and frightening feeling of loneliness. Mary knows even now the desolation of our hearts. She prays at this very moment for N., and for those left behind. Mary is our strength in times of trouble for she was not spared the pain either. She offers to us the wellspring of her own strength so that we might draw the water of hope from her fountain of faith.

Just as Mary was forced to give up her only Son to return to God the Father the great gift of life he gave to her in Jesus his Son, so too must we understand that no words will take away the pain or sorrow, no amount of reasoning will yield up adequate answers to the terrible and haunting question before our minds today. We must simply believe in God and draw the strength from his Holy Eucharist, allowing his ways to become our own.

There is a story in the Talmud which tells of a certain Rabbi and his wife who had two sons to whom they were extremely devoted. One Sabbath morning while the Rabbi was out teaching the law, both boys were struck by a sudden illness and died. Their mother laid them on a bed and covered them with a sheet. When the Rabbi came home for his meal and asked where the children were, his wife made some lame excuse and waited until the Rabbi had eaten.

She did not answer his question but instead asked one of him. "I am placed in a difficulty," she said, "because some time ago a person entrusted to my care some possession of great value which he now wants me to give back. Am I obliged to do this?"

"That you should need to put this question surprises me," the Rabbi replied, "since there can be no doubt. How can you hesitate to restore to everyone his own?" His wife then took the Rabbi back to the room where the two bodies lay and pulled back the sheet. "My sons, my sons," groaned the father in pain. "The Lord gave and the Lord has taken away," said the wife through her tears, "and you have always taught me to restore without reluctance that which has been lent to us for our happiness."

Funeral Homily for an Elderly Person

Longevity has always been considered a sign of God's favor. Our Hebrew forefathers in the faith looked upon old age as Yahweh's special blessing. The Psalmist of old continually spoke kindly and respectfully of what he termed "length of days," viewing old age as a golden gift bestowed upon the upright of heart. The author of the Book of Proverbs took pains to point out his feeling regarding the elderly; he wrote, "Gray hairs are a glorious crown which is worn by a righteous life." The tradition of our faith, the feelings of our renowned ancestors, the words of God's

Holy Book, all celebrate the bounty of our Lord's kindness as embodied in the long life of our loved ones.

We gather here today, before God's holy altar, assembled as we are in his sacred house, not to mourn for N., though sad we are, but to praise the Lord for allowing N. to have lived so long among us. Unlike the grief which attends to the passing of the young — those in the spring of their years — our heavy hearts are lightened today by the sure knowledge that our beloved has found favor with the Lord and is now at peace.

We will surely miss N.'s presence. We will all be the poorer for loss of his (her) wise counsel. He (she) enriched us immeasurably with his (her) faith while he (she) dwelt among us; now he (she) will plead our cause before the throne of God. He (she) shall speak gently in our name to our Lord Jesus Christ. At length N. will love us deeply yet as he (she) takes his (her) place at our Lord's heavenly banquet table.

To be sure, we feel sad that even in old age death must come; that we couldn't enjoy N.'s presence for yet a few more years. But God is God for those of us who pass on and for those of us who stay behind. The Lord will strengthen us, even as he strengthened and supported N. through these many years. Our sadness is real but not without hope for we live in faith, longing for the day when we will be reunited with our deceased, never again to be separated.

Today many thoughts pass through our minds and fond memories are recalled with tenderness. The task God gave to N. has been accomplished, but the work of the gospel continues on for us. Our beloved shared his (her) faith with us, nourished our beliefs and supported our decisions. The legacy of faith, hope and love is ours and we now must take up the task of living up to N.'s good name and righteous example.

Recall with me the story of Moses' death. Moses had lived a most eventful life and at length he grew old and weary; his strength failed him and God called Moses home just as he was about to lead his people into the promised land. Joshua, Moses' lieutenant, called out to the Lord, "Your servant Moses is dead"; and the Lord Yahweh spoke to Joshua, "Joshua, Joshua, arise and prepare for the task — lead my people home."

God calls out to us today, even as he spoke to Joshua of old; he asks us to continue the work N. began, to remain faithful to the gospel which N. lived with such telling effect. God has called our loved one home. He now calls us to persevere in the faith with a heart ablaze with love and hope. Recount your blessings today, recount the gift of N.'s life among us; recount, with still more profound fervor, God's glorious promise that one day the Church on earth and the Church in heaven will be completely one. Let us pray now with the Psalmist:

"Bless the Lord, O my soul, and all our being, bless his holy name. Bless the Lord, O my soul, and forget not all his benefits."

Public Celebration of Mass
for Deceased Separated Christians

On June 11, 1976, the Sacred Congregation for the Doctrine of the Faith issued a decree regarding the public celebration of holy Mass in the Catholic Church for other Christians who have died. In the opening paragraph the decree recognizes the growing practice of persons approaching the Catholic priest requesting a Mass to be celebrated for them. The reasons usually stem from a concern to pray liturgically for those who showed special devotion and honor for the Catholic religion or held a public office, which served all persons regardless of religious affiliations. Likewise for reasons of friendship, blood relations, etc., many Catholics and even Protestants (usually ones involved in a mixed marriage) approach a priest to say a Mass for a "Protestant."

This growing practice is probably a direct result of the ecumenical forces unleashed at Vatican II. Happily, Rome has responded favorably to the situation and now chooses a course which will only help to strengthen the historically weak links between Christians. Clearly, the celebration of Mass for a non-Catholic Christian is nothing new. The Code of Canon Law has always permitted such charity, but restricted this to the private sphere. What is new is that now Mass for non-Catholics may be celebrated *publicly*.

In the new decree the Sacred Congregation for the Doctrine of the Faith cites the prevailing Canon Law governing this matter. It recalls to our attention that the present canonical discipline states that Mass may be celebrated privately but not publicly for those who have passed on outside full communion with the Catholic Church. The decree states the following for taking up this question:

In view of the present change in the religious and social situation that gave rise to the above-mentioned discipline, the Sacred Congregation for the Doctrine of the Faith has received inquiries from various quarters to ask if in certain cases even public Masses can be celebrated for those deceased persons.

The Sacred Congregation for the Doctrine of the Faith decrees the following:

That the present discipline regarding the public celebration of holy Mass for other Christians who have passed away shall continue to be the general rule. The reason given for this is so as to respect the conscience of those who have died outside full communion who do not desire a public celebration of Mass for themselves.

So the general rule of the Code of Canon Law (private Mass, not public) is retained, but only on principle. By way of exception, the following is stated in the decree:

Exception can be allowed to this general rule, until the new Code is promulgated, whenever *both* the following are verified:

1. The request to celebrate Mass publicly for the deceased must be made explicitly by the relatives, friends or subjects of the deceased for a genuine religious motive. This simply means that there must be a specific request for a public Mass and that the public Mass must be sought for the spiritual good of the person (e.g., salvation) and not for reasons of public ostentation, or some similar secular reason.

2. In the judgment of the ordinary of the diocese there must be no scandal for the faithful. The term "ordinary" here is used broadly to include all persons who fall under the category of "ordinary" in Canon Law — Roman Pontiff, residential bishop within his territory, abbot, vicar general, administrator, vicar and prefect apostolic, those who succeed to office during a vacancy and in exempt clerical institutes, the major superior.

In each diocese the bishop and his curia should take immediate steps to establish a diocesan policy regarding this question. They ought to formally allow the decision whether or not to celebrate public Mass for deceased non-Catholics to rest with the pastor and his associates in the ministry. Since these ministers are in the best position to judge the potential for scandal, the decision in law ought to remain at the local pastoral level.

However, because the nature of the decree is essentially pastoral and ecumenical and because Canon Law allows pastoral decisions in urgent cases, it would appear that in individual cases the authorization of public Mass for non-Catholic Christians can rest with the pastor, always taking care to avoid scandal. The decree hastens to add that these two conditions are more easily verified in the case of our brothers in the Eastern Churches.

3. The Sacred Congregation for the Doctrine of the Faith informs us that when the above two conditions are verified, public Mass may be celebrated provided that the name of the deceased not be mentioned in the Eucharistic prayer. The reason given is this would presuppose full communion with the Catholic Church.

Pope Paul himself has repealed to whatever extent is necessary Canon 809 (along with Canon 2262, No. 2) and Canon 1241.

• *The Law of the Code*

The celebration of Mass for the living may be applied for the lawful intention of both a spiritual as well as a temporal nature, at the request of anyone — Catholic, non-Catholic or unbaptized. The emphasis is usually on Mass for the living. The Code allows a priest to apply private Mass, providing no scandal persists, even for the excommunicated (the Code here is referring to heretics and schismatics, two terms that are seldom employed today). However, in the case of those excommunicated *vitandi*, Mass may be said only for their conversion. This means that Mass may not be celebrated for any other intentions of the one excommunicated *vitandi*. Who are *vitandi*? Those who have by name been excommunicated by the Holy See, whose declaration is made public, and who in the decree itself are declared to be *vitandi*. Obviously, there are few *vitandi*.

The entire matter has been temporarily resolved by the enlightened pastoral regulation emanating from the Holy See. They are temporary only insofar as they await full incorporation into the new Code of Canon Law, now under revision.

This decree is a welcome aid to the priest in his parochial ministry, especially regarding questions of Christian burial, cremation, etc. The new regulation augments the previous pastoral discipline surrounding the liturgy for a deceased. Of course it has always been considered highly questionable to dub the celebration of the Eucharist (Mass) private and public. The rather hazy distinction drawn between "public Mass" and "private Mass" (apart from the apparent character of the celebration) has left the law a bit hollow in this regard and actually is theologically untenable. There is but one *Mass* and the fruits of its celebration and those for whom it is able to be celebrated ought always to be understood as identical whether the Mass is in chapel or church.

In summary, the new law states:

Public celebration of Mass for deceased non-Catholic Christians may take place if it is explicitly requested for a genuine spiritual motive, and no chance of scandal exists.

One further note: The best way to cancel the possibility of scandal is to educate the people of God. If this decree of the Holy See is made known to the parishioners and explained, it will go a long way to prevent any wonderment over a public Mass for a "Protestant."

Final Commendation and Farewell When Celebrated in Church After Mass

IN THE CHURCH

After the prayer after Communion, the priest, vested in a chasuble or cope, begins the rite of final commendation and farewell.

The priest stands near the coffin with the ministers who have the holy water and incense. If the body was sprinkled with holy water at the entrance to the church at the beginning of Mass, the sprinkling is ordinarily omitted in the rite of commendation. If the body was incensed at the preparation of the gifts during Mass, the incensation is ordinarily omitted in the rite of commendation. He faces the people and introduces the rite in these or similar words:

• FORM "A" •

PRIEST

With faith in Jesus Christ,
we reverently bring the body of our brother (sister)
to be buried in its human imperfection.

Let us pray with confidence to God,
who gives life to all things,
that he will raise up this mortal body
to the perfection and the company of the saints.

May God give him (her) a merciful judgment
and forgive all his (her) sins.
May Christ, the Good Shepherd,
lead him (her) safely home
to be at peace with God our Father.
And may he (she) be happy for ever
with all the saints
in the presence of the eternal King.

• FORM "B" •

PRIEST

Our brother (sister) has gone to his (her) rest in the peace of Christ. With faith and hope in eternal life, let us

commend him (her) to the loving mercy of our Father, and assist him (her) with our prayers. He (she) became God's son (daughter) through baptism and was often fed at the table of our Lord. May the Lord now welcome him (her) to the table of God's children in heaven, and, with all the saints, may he (she) inherit the promise of eternal life.

Let us also pray to the Lord for ourselves. May we who mourn be reunited one day with our brother (sister). Together may we meet Christ Jesus when he, who is our life, shall appear in his glory.

Then all pray in silence for a little while.
If not done earlier in the Mass, the body is sprinkled with holy water and incensed, or this may be done after the song of farewell. If there is no singing, the invocations [below] may be said.

SONG OF
FAREWELL
(OR FORM "A")

V. Saints of God, come to his (her) aid!
Come to meet him (her), angels of the Lord!

R. Receive his (her) soul and present him (her) to God the Most High.

V. May Christ, who called you, take you to himself;
may angels lead you to Abraham's side.

R. Receive his (her) soul and present him (her) to God the Most High.

V. Give him (her) eternal rest, O Lord,

191

and may your light shine on him (her)
for ever.

R. Receive his (her) soul and present him
(her) to God the Most High.

RESPONSORY
(OR FORM "B")

PRIEST I know that my Redeemer lives, and
on the last day I shall rise again; in my
body I shall look on God, my Savior.

ALL I know that my Redeemer lives, and
on the last day I shall rise again; in my
body I shall look on God, my Savior.

PRIEST I myself shall see him; my own eyes
will gaze on him.

ALL In my body I shall look on God, my
Savior.

PRIEST This is the hope I cherish in my heart.

ALL In my body I shall look on God, my
Savior.

PRIEST AND ALL I know that my Redeemer lives, and
on the last day I shall rise again; in my
body I shall look on God, my Savior.

INVOCATIONS By your coming as man, *Lord, save
your people.*

[After each invocation, respond with:
Lord, save your people.]

By your birth,
By your baptism and fasting,
By your sufferings and cross,
By your death and burial,
By your rising to new life,
By your return in glory to the Father,
By your gift of the Holy Spirit,
By your coming again in glory, . . .

192

• FORM "A" •

PRIEST Father,
into your hands we commend our
            brother (sister).
We are confident that with all who
            have died in Christ
he (she) will be raised to life on the
            last day
and live with Christ for ever.
(We thank you for all the blessings
you gave him [her] in this life
to show your fatherly care for all of us
and the fellowship which is ours with
            the saints
in Jesus Christ.)
Lord, hear our prayer:
welcome our brother (sister) to para-
            dise
and help us to comfort each other
with the assurance of our faith
(until we all meet in Christ
to be with you and with our brother
            [sister] for ever).
(We ask this) through Christ our Lord.

ALL Amen.

• FORM "B" •

PRIEST We commend our brother (sister) N.
            to you, Lord.
Now that he (she) has passed from
            this life,
may he (she) live on in your presence.
In your mercy and love,
forgive whatever sins he (she) may
            have committed
through human weakness.
(We ask this) through Christ our Lord.

ALL Amen.

193

After the prayer, while the body is being taken away, one of the following antiphons may be sung:

• FORM "A" •
PRIEST

**May the angels lead you into paradise;
may the martyrs come to welcome
you
and take you to the holy city,
the new and eternal Jerusalem.**

• FORM "B" •
PRIEST

**May the choir of angels welcome you.
Where Lazarus is poor no longer,
may you have eternal rest.**

• FORM "C" •
PRIEST

**I am the resurrection and the life.
The man who believes in me will live
even if he dies,
and every living person
who puts faith in me
will never suffer eternal death.**

Psalms or other appropriate verses may be sung with these antiphons.

PROCESSION TO THE CEMETERY

During the procession to the cemetery, appropriate hymns may be sung.

AT THE GRAVE

If the grave or tomb has not been blessed, it is blessed before the body is placed in it. The priest says:

PRIEST

**Let us pray.
Lord Jesus Christ,
by the three days you lay in the tomb
you made holy the graves of all who
believe in you;
and even though their bodies lie in the
earth,
they trust that they, like you, will rise
again.**

194

Give our brother (sister) peaceful rest
in this grave,
until that day when you,
the resurrection and the life,
will raise him (her) up in glory.
Then may he (she) see the light of
your presence,
Lord Jesus,
in the kingdom where you live for ever
and ever.

ALL   Amen.

If not done earlier in the burial rite, the priest
may sprinkle and incense the body and the
grave or tomb.
Then the priest may say, in whole or in part,
the following prayer of the faithful, or a similar one:

PRIEST   Let us pray for our brother (sister)
to our Lord Jesus Christ,
who said:
"I am the resurrection and the life.
The man who believes in me will live
even if he dies,
and every living person
who puts his faith in me
will never suffer eternal death."
Lord, you wept at the death of Lazarus, your friend:
comfort us in our sorrow.
We ask this in faith:

ALL   Lord, hear our prayer.

PRIEST   You raise the dead to life:
give our brother (sister) eternal
life.
We ask this in faith:

ALL   Lord, hear our prayer.

PRIEST You promised paradise to the thief
        who repented:
              bring our brother (sister) to the
              joys of heaven.
        We ask this in faith:

ALL   Lord, hear our prayer.

PRIEST Our brother (sister) was washed clean
        in baptism
              and anointed with the oil of salva-
              tion:
              give him (her) fellowship with all
              your saints.
        We ask this in faith:

ALL   Lord, hear our prayer.

PRIEST He (she) was nourished with your body
        and blood:
              grant him (her) a place at the
              table in your heavenly king-
              dom.
        We ask this in faith:

ALL   Lord, hear our prayer.

PRIEST Comfort us in our sorrow at the death
        of our brother (sister):
              let our faith be our consolation
              and eternal life our hope.
        We ask this in faith:

ALL   Lord, hear our prayer.

Then all say the Lord's Prayer together, or the
priest says the following prayer:

PRIEST **Almighty God,**
        through the death of your Son on the
        cross,
        you have overcome death for us.
        Through his burial and resurrection
        from the dead

196

you have made the grave a holy place
and restored to us eternal life.
We pray for those who died believing
in Jesus
and are buried with him in the hope of
rising again.
God of the living and the dead,
may those who faithfully believed in
you on earth
praise you for ever in the joy of heav-
en.
(We ask this) through Christ our Lord.

ALL **Amen.**

In the United States, if a prayer for those present is desired, one of the following may be
added:

• FORM "A" •
PRIEST Let us pray,
God of all consolation,
in your unending love and mercy for us
you turn the darkness of death
into the dawn of new life.

Show compassion to your people in
sorrow.
(Be our refuge and our strength
to lift us from the darkness of this
grief
to the peace and light of your presence.)

Your Son, our Lord Jesus Christ,
by dying for us, conquered death
and by rising again, restored life.

May we then go forward eagerly to
meet him,
and after our life on earth
be reunited with our brothers and sisters

where every tear will be wiped away.
(We ask this) through Christ our Lord.

ALL   Amen.

• FORM "B" •
PRIEST   Lord Jesus,
our Redeemer,
you willingly gave yourself up to death
so that all people might be saved
and pass from death into a new life.
Listen to our prayers,
look with love on your people
who mourn and pray for their dead
   brother (sister).
Lord Jesus, you alone are holy and
   compassionate:
forgive our brother (sister) his (her)
   sins.
By dying you opened the gates of life
for those who believe in you:
do not let our brother (sister) be parted from you,
but by your glorious power
give him (her) light, joy, and peace in
   heaven
where you live for ever and ever.

ALL   Amen.

V.   Give him (her) eternal rest, O Lord.

R.   And may your light shine on him (her)
   forever.

If the body is lowered into the grave at this
time, the priest may say the following prayer:

PRIEST   Since almighty God has called our
   brother (sister) N.
from this life to himself,

198

we commit his (her) body
to the earth from which it was made.

Christ was the first to rise from the
dead,
and we know that he will raise up our
mortal bodies
to be like his in glory.

We commend our brother (sister) to
the Lord:
may the Lord receive him (her) into
his peace
and raise up his (her) body on the last
day.

At the end of the entire rite, an appropriate
song may be sung, according to local custom.

Final Commendation and Farewell
When Omitted in Church

AT THE GRAVE   If the grave or tomb has not been blessed, it is
blessed before the body is placed in it. The
priest says:

PRIEST   Lord God, through your mercy
those who have lived in faith
find eternal peace.
Bless this grave
and send your angel to watch over it.
Forgive the sins of our brother (sister)
whose body we bury here.
Welcome him (her) into your presence,
and with your saints let him (her) rejoice in you for ever.
(We ask this) through Christ our Lord.

ALL   Amen.

The priest stands near the coffin with the ministers who have the holy water and incense.

PRIEST   Our brother (sister) has gone to his (her) rest in the peace of Christ. With faith and hope in eternal life, let us commend him (her) to the loving mercy of our Father, and assist him (her) with our prayers. He (she) became God's son (daughter) through baptism and was often fed at the table of our Lord. May the Lord now welcome him (her) to the table of God's children in heaven, and, with all the saints, may he (she) inherit the promise of eternal life.

Let us also pray to the Lord for ourselves. May we who mourn be reunited one day with our brother (sister). Together may we meet Christ when he, who is our life, shall appear in his glory.

Then all pray in silence for a little while.
A reading from Scripture, and a responsorial psalm may then be said, especially if there is some interval between the station in the church and the burial.

PRIEST   *A Reading From the Gospel According to John (12:23-26)*
Jesus said:
"The hour has come
for the Son of Man to be glorified.
I solemnly assure you,
unless the grain of wheat falls to the earth and dies,
it remains just a grain of wheat.
But if it dies,
it produces much fruit.
The man who loves his life loses it,

while the man who hates his life in this
world
preserves it to life eternal.
If anyone would serve me,
let him follow me;
where I am,
there will my servant be.
If anyone serves me,
him the Father will honor.''

RESPONSORIAL
PSALM

PSALM 93   If used antiphonally, use the following response.

R.   Of earth you formed me, with flesh
you covered me; Lord, my Redeemer,
raise me up again at the last day.

V.   The Lord is king, in splendor robed;
robed is the Lord and girt about
with strength;
And he has made the world firm,
not to be moved.

R.   Of earth you formed me, with flesh
you covered me; Lord, my Redeemer,
raise me up again at the last day.

V.   Your throne stands firm from of old;
from everlasting you are, O Lord.

R.   Of earth you formed me, with flesh
you covered me; Lord, my Redeemer,
raise me up again at the last day.

V.   The floods lift up, O Lord, the floods
lift up their voice;
the floods lift up their tumult.
More powerful than the roar of many
waters,
more powerful than the breakers
of the sea —
powerful on high is the Lord.

R. Of earth you formed me, with flesh you covered me; Lord, my Redeemer, raise me up again at the last day.

V. Your decrees are worthy of trust indeed:
   holiness befits your house, O Lord, for length of days.

R. Of earth you formed me, with flesh you covered me; Lord, my Redeemer, raise me up again at the last day.

The body is sprinkled with holy water and incensed, or this may be done after the song of farewell. If there is no singing, the invocations [below] may be said.

SONG OF
FAREWELL

V. Saints of God, come to his (her) aid!
   Come to meet him (her), angels of the Lord!

R. Receive his (her) soul and present him (her) to God the Most High.

V. May Christ, who called you, take you to himself;
   may angels lead you to Abraham's side.

R. Receive his (her) soul and present him (her) to God the Most High.

V. Give him (her) eternal rest, O Lord, and may your light shine on him (her) for ever.

R. Receive his (her) soul and present him (her) to God the Most High.

INVOCATIONS By your coming as man, *Lord, save your people.*

[After each invocation, respond with:
Lord, save your people.]

By your birth,
By your baptism and fasting,
By your sufferings and cross,
By your death and burial,
By your rising to new life,
By your return in glory to the Father,
By your gift of the Holy Spirit,
By your coming again in glory, . . .

Then the priest says the following prayer:

• FORM "A" •

PRIEST Father,
into your hands we commend our
    brother (sister).
We are confident that with all who
    have died in Christ
he (she) will be raised to life on the
    last day
and live with Christ for ever.
(We thank you for all the blessings
you gave him [her] in this life
to show your fatherly care for all of us
and the fellowship which is ours with
    the saints
in Jesus Christ.)
Lord, hear our prayer:
welcome our brother (sister) to para-
    dise
and help us to comfort each other
with the assurance of our faith
(until we all meet in Christ
to be with you and with our brother
    [sister] for ever).
(We ask this) through Christ our Lord.

ALL Amen.

PRIEST   We commend our brother (sister) N. to you, Lord.
Now that he (she) has passed from this life,
may he (she) live on in your presence.
In your mercy and love,
forgive whatever sins he (she) may have committed
through human weakness.
(We ask this) through Christ our Lord.

ALL   Amen.

In the United States, if a prayer for those present is desired, the following prayer may be added:

PRIEST   Let us pray.
Lord Jesus,
our Redeemer,
you willingly gave yourself up to death
so that all people might be saved
and pass from death into a new life.
Listen to our prayers,
look with love on your people
who mourn and pray for their dead brother (sister).
Lord Jesus, you alone are holy and compassionate:
forgive our brother (sister) his (her) sins.
By dying you opened the gates of life
for those who believe in you:
do not let our brother (sister) be parted from you,
but by your glorious power
give him (her) light, joy, and peace in heaven
where you live for ever and ever.

204

ALL   Amen.

V.   Give him (her) eternal rest, O Lord.

R.   And may your light shine on him (her) forever.

At the end of the entire rite, an appropriate song may be sung, according to local custom.

14

Cremation and Christian Burial

The Catholic Church has always been of the mind that cremation is alien to a proper understanding of the sacredness of the body. The Church reasoned that, because of the sacred character of human life, founded in a most profound way upon the incarnation of Jesus, no Christian — but especially Catholic — ought even to entertain the idea of cremation, lest he should find himself disrespecting the body. Because of the long-standing tradition within the Church of proper interment, namely the custom of burying the dead in holy (consecrated) ground, there was relatively little desire on the part of the people to seek to have their bodies or those of loved ones cremated.

This venerable tradition and practice of burying the dead was supported theologically by the belief that "to do violence" to the body somehow ran counter to the proper and accurate understanding of bodily resurrection. Coupled with this was the reaction against certain pagan customs, which either mutilated the dead or cremated them on funeral pyres. Since it was unheard of for a Catholic to consider cremation, and since the penalty for violation was generally denial of Christian burial, the custom of proscribing cremation obtained the force of law by virtue of consent of the faithful. Furthermore, until recently, there existed no overriding need to employ cremation since cemetery ground abounded.

The cremation of bodies during disease-ridden periods of epidemics (e.g., plague) was a practical and essential response to a particularly dire situation. Of course the Church recognized the need for exception to the law prohibiting cremation during time of local or national emergency when public welfare demanded employing this form of burial. Likewise, the Church has allowed, for some time, cremation of amputated limbs (Decree of the Holy Office, August 3, 1897). But what of the cremation of bodies apart from extraordinary circumstances and dire need? Just where does Church law now stand regarding cremation of the body?

In a document issued by the Sacred Congregation for the Sacraments and Divine Worship, dated August 15, 1969, entitled *Ordo Exsequiarum* (Order of Funeral Services), a notable change in the Church's stand on cremation is evidenced. The section of the document which concerns our topic can be found in the *Praenotanda*, No. 15. It serves as a pastoral application of the law as advanced in previous documents. What this document does is to remove many of the earlier restrictions, except those cases in which cremation is opted for as an "anti-Christian gesture." The new directives contained in *Ordo Exsequiarum* take precedence over any and all previous norms in force up till now. The Church, in this document, has tempered its stand on cremation.

The new document states: "The Christian funeral service is to be given to those who have chosen cremation of their own body, unless it is certain that in making such a choice they were motivated by reasons hostile to the Christian life in accordance with what has been laid down in the instruction of the Holy Office dated May 8, 1963, *De Cadaverum Crematione,* Nos. 2-3."

"The Christian funeral service *is to be given* to those who have chosen cremation . . . *unless* . . ." Thus the law is changed to allow a Christian to opt for cremation, without penalty, provided his motives are not the mocking of the Christian belief in the sacredness of the body or resurrection, or to signify something anti-Christian. The right to choose cremation is given here. While the penalty in Canon Law to cremation as a sign of defiance still stands, good faith and sincere motives for choosing cremation is imputed to the faithful unless the contrary is implied and proven.

The document goes on to say: "The funeral rites are to be celebrated according to the form in use in the region but in such a way that one does not obscure the fact that the Church prefers the custom of burial in imitation of the Lord himself."

Can the priest go to the crematorium and preside over the final obsequies? The answer is yes. The document states: "The rites which are performed in the cemetery chapel or at the graveside itself, in this case, can be carried out in the chapel of the crematorium itself; and if there is no other suitable place, even in the room where the cremator is situated, provided always that there is no real danger of scandal or religious indifferentism." One can readily see how softened is the tone of Rome in this matter. Truly, the Holy See is providing for a pastoral need in a most understanding manner — especially given the long-standing tradition to the contrary. It is clear that these norms indicate a shift in the Church's official position regarding cremation. Moreover, these norms further indicate that the Church is no longer actively or positively opposed to the practice of cremation — except when cremation is used as a hostile sign to our belief. (Permission to be cremated need not be requested.)

The priest confronted with the decision for cremation ought to conduct the regular rite of the Church for the deceased, as usual: namely, the resurrection liturgy with the homily stressing the nature of our belief in eternal life and resurrection, coupled with the service at the crematorium. This liturgical rite should be conducted as if at the graveside with appropriate alterations in text to adapt the ceremony to the circumstance of cremation.

(A pastoral suggestion: It would be most appropriate for the priest to exhort the family to have the remains of the deceased buried in the usual manner. The custom of sprinkling the ashes over the countryside or over open water ought to be discouraged. In fact, this practice is not in keeping with the spirit of Christian burial. One can go too far in the name of pastoral concern.)

The priest may suggest that the family bring the body into church in an inexpensive casket, and conduct the Eucharist and the traditional funeral liturgy. Cremation can take place after the church services and the burial of the ashes at a later date. Another suggestion, which is a custom followed in some places, is to bring the urn of the ashes to the church and place it in the center aisle on an appropriate and suitable table with the lighted paschal candle. The Eucharist and the customary prayers of commendation are conducted as if the casket were present. Burial takes place at the cemetery with the usual prayers.

One final note: The law in force regarding the denial of Christian burial to those living outside the law of God or his Church is: Ecclesiastical burial shall not be denied to manifest sinners, if, before death, they gave some sign of penance and there is no public scandal to the faithful. This means simply that everyone is to be given a Christian burial unless they have flaunted their extra-ecclesial status, request cremation as a sign hostile to Christian belief, or serious public scandal can be expected to emanate from a public Church burial. If it is evident or proven that the deceased actually requested cremation as a means of showing hostility to the Catholic Church, or for the purpose of denying Christian dogma, or for any other anti-Christian motive, then it seems that the penalty of privation of Church burial is incurred, even if the order to cremate is not carried out by the deceased's family.

However, in the event that the family of the deceased, apart from his or her desire, has the body cremated because of any of the above hostile reasons, or out of contempt for the Church, it appears that Church burial can be granted to the deceased, so long as care is taken to avoid all possibility of scandal. Simply stated, the deceased must not be penalized for the sins of his or her family. Justice must always prevail.

Pastoral care must be taken to instruct the faithful on the laws of the Church. This is especially incumbent upon priests when cases or situations are those in which public scandal or amazement is likely to arise, thus confusing the people as to where the Church stands on certain matters. Clearly, as the population increases and land for burial decreases, the request for cremation will become even more frequent. Owing to this future need to resort to cremation as a means of burial (perhaps the ordinary means), those in a position to educate the faithful ought to take the necessary time to communicate the legitimacy of cremation, but never at the expense of relegating Christian burial to an inferior position. However, the customary Christian obsequies ought always to be preferred over cremation.

15

Blessings for Persons, Places and Things

Never pay back one wrong with another,
or an angry word with another one;
instead, pay back with a blessing.
That is what you are called to do,
so that you inherit a blessing yourself.

— *(1 Peter 3:9)*

In March 1972, the Congregation for the Sacraments and Divine Worship summarized its thoughts on blessings:

• Blessings obtain certain spiritual effects. They bless men and things, or pray for men and their needs.

• The first element in a blessing is thanksgiving and praise toward God (as in the *berakah* prayers used over bread and wine during the preparation of the gifts at Mass).

• A blessing recognizes and proclaims that creation is good, and that our Creator looks after us in his providential love. When man gives thanks at various moments in his life, he recognizes and professes that all things have been made by God and come to us from him.

• The use of blessings should increase in the lives of Christians; we ought to continue to advert to God and to his constant guidance of the universe. To help bring this about, it is good to extend the use of blessings to lay persons, especially blessings which belong to their daily life and work.

• Blessings which belong directly to worship are reserved for use by an ordained minister.

Blessing of Love
(Attributed to St. Francis)

Lord, make us instruments of your peace.
Where there is hatred, let us sow love;
Where there is injury, pardon;
Where there is discord, union;
Where there is doubt, faith;
Where there is despair, hope;

Where there is darkness, light;
Where there is sadness, joy.
Grant that we may not so much seek to be consoled as to console;
To be understood as to understand;
To be loved as to love.
For it is in giving that we receive,
It is in pardoning that we are pardoned,
And it is in dying that we are born to eternal life. Amen.

Prayers for Peace

PRIEST: Our help is in the name of the Lord.
PEOPLE: Who made heaven and earth.
PRIEST: The Lord be with you.
PEOPLE: And also with you.

Let us pray.

• God our Father, you reveal that those who work for peace will be called your sons. Help us to work without ceasing for that justice which brings true and everlasting peace. We ask this through Christ our Lord. Amen.

• God, Creator of the world, you established the order which governs all ages. Hear our prayer and give us peace in our time that we may rejoice in your mercy and praise you without end. We ask this through Jesus, your Son and our Lord. Amen.

• God of perfect peace, neither violence nor cruelty can be a part of you. May those who are at peace with one another hold fast to the good will that unites them. May those who are enemies forget their hatred and be healed. Grant this peace to all men throughout the world. Amen.

• Lord Jesus Christ, we praise you; bring peace into the world by bringing your peace into the hearts of men. Help us to turn away from sin, and to follow you in love and service. Glory and honor be yours for ever and ever. Amen.

Thanksgiving

PRIEST: Our help is in the name of the Lord.
PEOPLE: Who made heaven and earth.
PRIEST: The Lord be with you.
PEOPLE: And also with you.

Let us pray.

• Father of all gifts, we praise you, the source of all we have and are. Teach us to acknowledge always the good things your infinite love has given us. Help us to love you with all our hearts and all our strength as our expression of thanksgiving for your many blessings. Fill our hearts with this spirit of gratitude. Amen.

• Father of mercy, we thank you for your kindness and ask you to free us from all evil that we may serve you with generous hearts and in happiness all our days. Make us always aware of your mercies that with truly thankful hearts, we may make known your praise by giving wholeheartedly of ourselves, and by true holiness of lives all honor and glory will be yours throughout all ages. Amen.

• Almighty God, Father of all mercies, we your unworthy servants give you humble thanks for all your goodness and loving kindness to us and to all men. We bless you for our creation and all the blessings of this life, but above all, for your incomparable and undying love in the redemption of the world by your Son, our Lord and Savior Jesus Christ. Amen.

• Heavenly Father, we your unworthy servants give you humble thanks for all your goodness and loving kindness to us and to all men, particularly our families, friends and loved ones.

We thank you for all the blessings of this life, our disappointments and failures, but above all, for your incomparable love in the redemption of the world, through your Son Jesus Christ, and for the means of grace and the hope of glory.

Make us always aware of your mercies, so that with thankful hearts we may make known your praise, not only with our lips but in our lives, by giving of ourselves to your service. May others see you in us by the charity and holiness of our lives.

Grant us the gift of your Spirit, so that we can know him and make him known; and through him, at all times and in all places, we may give thanks to you in all things. Amen.

For Our Fellowmen

PRIEST: Our help is in the name of the Lord.
PEOPLE: Who made heaven and earth.
PRIEST: The Lord be with you.
PEOPLE: And also with you.

Let us pray.

• O God, you have made us in your likeness and redeemed us through your Son Jesus Christ. Look with compassion on all of our fellowmen throughout the world. Take away arrogance and hatred from our hearts. Bless us abundantly, so that in your good time all nations and peoples may serve you in peace and harmony here and around your heavenly throne. We ask this through Jesus Christ our Lord. Amen.

Grace at Meals

PRIEST: Our help is in the name of the Lord.
PEOPLE: Who made heaven and earth.
PRIEST: The Lord be with you.
PEOPLE: And also with you.

Let us pray.

• Bless us, O Lord, and these your gifts which we are about to receive from your bounty and goodness through Christ our Lord. Amen.

• Heavenly Father, make us grateful for all your mercies and make us ever mindful of the needs of others, especially those less fortunate and blessed. Amen.

• Lord God, King of the universe, you give us food to sustain our lives and bless us in so many ways. Help us never to forget your love and providential care. Amen.

• Father in heaven, we praise you for giving us your Son to be our Savior and Lord. Bless us as we gather together and let us always live in your love. Fill our hearts with a deep spirit of love. Hear our prayer, loving Father, for we ask this in Jesus' name. Amen.

• Blessed be your name, our God and our Provider, for the gifts of this nation, this land, and for our table. Bring us together in this sharing. Like the supper of Jesus, let this occasion nourish us with faith in you, with care for one another, and with food to give us pleasure and to make us strong. We know that we dare thank you only if our sharing reaches out to all in need. Amen.

• *Greek Orthodox:* Blessed be God, who in his mercy nourishes us from his bounteous gifts by his grace and compassion. O Christ, our God, bless the meat and drink of which we are about to partake, for you are holy forever. Amen.

• *Protestant:* Bless, O Lord, this food for our use, and us for your service, and make us ever mindful of the needs of others, in Jesus' name. Amen.

• *Jewish:* Lift up your hands toward the sanctuary and bless the Lord. Blessed are you, O Lord our God, King of the universe, who brings forth bread from the earth. Amen.

214

Special Prayer for Thanksgiving Day

• O God, you have fulfilled our founding fathers' faith in your divine providence by making and keeping us a land rich in the abundance of your creation. Freedom, justice and universal brotherhood are for us our precious heritage, but for countless men, in our midst and all over the world, they are still only a dream. May we be faithful in sharing this heritage with the living and transmit it to a people still unborn. We ask this through our Lord Jesus Christ, your Son, who lives and reigns with you and the Holy Spirit, one God, for ever and ever. Amen.

Wedding Banquet

(A form of grace that may be used at the beginning of a wedding banquet.)

• My friends, let us pray. *(All pause for a moment of silent prayer.)*

Dear Father of us all, we praise you and give you glory today. We thank you for the gifts you have shown to us; for the love you have given to N. and N.; for the joy we are sharing; and for this wedding banquet we are about to begin. Bless us, Father, and the food we eat, and make us truly grateful for all your gifts. We praise you through Christ our Lord. Amen.

For Our Enemies

PRIEST:	Our help is in the name of the Lord.
PEOPLE:	Who made heaven and earth.
PRIEST:	The Lord be with you.
PEOPLE:	And also with you.

Let us pray.

• O God of all mankind, whose Son commands us to love those who hate us, hear our prayers for our enemies. Deliver them and us from deeds beneath the dignity of man whom you have redeemed. Turn us from our evil ways by removing hatred, cruelty and revenge from our hearts. Let others see Christ in us, and that we reflect his love in every thought, word and action. Amen.

For the Church

(May be used for the diocese and the parish.)

PRIEST: Our help is in the name of the Lord.

PEOPLE: Who made heaven and earth.

PRIEST: The Lord be with you.

PEOPLE: And also with you.

Let us pray.

• Gracious Father, hear our prayers for your holy Catholic Church. Fill it with truth and keep it in your peace. Strengthen and confirm its members, and grant them every blessing that they be of one heart and one mind. Where it is in error, correct it. Where it is in want, provide for it. Where it is divided, reunite it. Where it is right, strengthen and defend it. We ask this for the sake of your Son, our Savior Jesus Christ. Amen.

• O God, sustain your Church as it faces new tasks in the distress and confusions of this rapidly changing world. Let your Holy Spirit guide our Holy Father the Pope, our bishops and our priests with sound judgment, convictions and the strength to persevere in being bold witness to your kingdom on earth. We ask this through Jesus Christ our Lord. Amen.

For Church Unity

PRIEST: Our help is in the name of the Lord.

PEOPLE: Who made heaven and earth.

PRIEST: The Lord be with you.

PEOPLE: And also with you.

Let us pray.

• Lord Jesus Christ, you said to your apostles, "Peace I give you; my own peace I leave with you." Regard not our sins, but the faith of your Church. Take away all hatred and prejudice and whatever else may hinder us from unity. May we all be of one heart and one soul united in one holy bond of truth and peace, of faith and love, so that we may with one mind and one tongue sing out your glory. We ask this through Jesus Christ our Lord. Amen.

For Our Country

PRIEST: Our help is in the name of the Lord.

PEOPLE: Who made heaven and earth.

PRIEST: The Lord be with you.

PEOPLE: And also with you.

Let us pray.

• Almighty God, we humbly thank you for this good land which you have given us for our inheritance. We pray that we may always prove to be a people mindful of your love and kindness. Bless this land with honest labor. Save us from violence, discord and confusion, from pride and arrogance, and from every evil way. Preserve and increase our liberties, and fashion into one united nation this people of many races and tongues. Fill with the spirit of wisdom those to whom we entrust the authority of government, that they may seek justice and peace. In time of prosperity, fill our hearts with thankfulness and in time of trouble, do not allow our trust and hope in you to fail. All this we ask through Jesus Christ our Lord. Amen.

For Civil Authorities

PRIEST: Our help is in the name of the Lord.
PEOPLE: Who made heaven and earth.
PRIEST: The Lord be with you.
PEOPLE: And also with you.

Let us pray.

• O Lord, the whole world is full of your glory. We commend our country to your merciful care, that we may follow your guidance and live in peace. Give to the President of these United States [or governor of this state, etc.], and to all authority, wisdom and strength to know and to do your holy will. Fill them with the love of truth, honesty and righteousness. Make them always remember that they are your servants called to lead and serve this nation [or state, etc.] in the fear of your righteous judgments. Through Jesus Christ our Lord, who lives and governs with you and the Holy Spirit, one God, now and forever. Amen.

For Congress or a State Legislature

PRIEST: Our help is in the name of the Lord.
PEOPLE: Who made heaven and earth.
PRIEST: The Lord be with you.
PEOPLE: And also with you.

Let us pray.

• O God, the source of all wisdom, whose statutes are good and gracious, and whose law is truth, guide and direct our senators and congressmen [or state legislature, etc.], that by just and prudent laws, they may promote the well-being of all our people. Through Christ our Lord. Amen.

• Almighty God, our Father, you have charged us with the task of building on this earth a home where all the nations dwell in unity, liberty and justice. We pray for strength and purpose to make officers in every branch of government accountable to all the people, fulfilling roles of service and responsibility, that they may seek justice and protect the weak and lead us in constructing institutions for our peace and mutual aid. Amen.

For Social Justice

PRIEST: Our help is in the name of the Lord.

PEOPLE: Who made heaven and earth.

PRIEST: The Lord be with you.

PEOPLE: And also with you.

Let us pray.

• Almighty God, you have created us in your own image. Grant us strength and courage to fearlessly contend against evil, that we may rightly use our freedom and have strong convictions to be counted when we are put to the test. Help us employ the principles of freedom and Christian ideals in the struggle for justice among men and nations, to the glory of your holy name. Through Jesus Christ our Lord. Amen.

• Grant, O Lord, your holy and life-giving Spirit that every human heart may be moved and promoted to break through the barriers that divide the peoples of our land. Destroy the spirit of hatred; and may suspicions disappear and hatreds cease, so that we may live in justice and peace for which Christ gave his life that all men would be saved. Amen.

• In the midst of our complex and hurried lives, our Father, remind us of our simple roots. We have to carry about so much and manage so many things, that we dare not be distracted by our neighbor. If we do not reach out to others, it is not because we do not want to, but because our arms are tired from grasping, holding, keeping all the good things we possess. Lighten our load, so that we may learn to share; and help us learn to share, so that our load may be lightened. Amen.

For Those in the Armed Forces

PRIEST: Our help is in the name of the Lord.

PEOPLE: Who made heaven and earth.

PRIEST: The Lord be with you.

PEOPLE: And also with you.

Let us pray.

• Heavenly Father, we commend to your gracious and protective care and benevolent keeping all the men and women of our armed forces at home and abroad. Defend them day by day with your guiding hand and heavenly grace; encourage them and strengthen them in their trials, temptations and discouragements; grant them your abiding presence wherever they may be. We ask this through Christ our Lord. Amen.

Blessing of a School

PRIEST: Our help is in the name of the Lord.
PEOPLE: Who made heaven and earth.
PRIEST: The Lord be with you.
PEOPLE: And also with you.

Let us pray.

• Lord Jesus Christ, sanctify, we implore you, this building meant for the education of children. Pour into it the richness of your blessing and peace. Nurture your children with Christian ideals. Enlighten with your wisdom those who teach and those who learn, that rejoicing together in the knowledge of your truth, we may worship and serve you from generation to generation. Through Jesus Christ our Lord. Amen.

For Schools and Colleges

• O God, the source of all truth, behold with your gracious favor our schools and colleges that knowledge and wisdom may be increased among us. Bless all who teach and all who learn, that their minds will be open to the truths of Christian ideals and principles. Bless both teacher and student that they may ever look to you their God, the source of all truth, and accept your teachings in genuine humility of heart. Amen.

Blessing for an Elderly Person

PRIEST: Our help is in the name of the Lord.
PEOPLE: Who made heaven and earth.
PRIEST: The Lord be with you.
PEOPLE: And also with you.

Let us pray.

• Father in heaven, remember those who have grown old in your love and service. Bless them and give them strength; keep them in your love. Give them your joy and peace each day, so that they may always follow your Son Jesus. Amen.

For the Sick

PRIEST: Our help is in the name of the Lord.

PEOPLE: Who made heaven and earth.

PRIEST: The Lord be with you.

PEOPLE: And also with you.

Let us pray.

• Father, your Son accepted our sufferings to teach us the virtue of patience in human illness. Hear the prayers we offer for our sick friends and relatives. May all who suffer from disease or painful lingering sicknesses realize that they are chosen to be saints, and know that they are joined to Christ in his suffering for the salvation of the world, who lives and reigns with you and the Holy Spirit, one God, for ever and ever. Amen.

• Heavenly Father, our help in human weakness, show our sick and suffering friends the power of your loving care. Accept the prayers and gifts we offer for them. In your kindness make them well, and if it is your will, restore them to health and turn our society for them into joy. We ask this in the name of Jesus the Lord. Amen.

• Heavenly Father, your love guides every moment of our lives. Accept our prayers and petitions for our sick relative [or friend, etc.], N.; restore his (her) health and turn our anxiety for him (her) into joy. We ask this in the name of Jesus the Lord. Amen.

• Merciful Father, giver of life and health, bless N., your servant, and those who minister to him (her) your healing gifts that he (she) may be restored to complete health and render to you prayers and gratitude. Through Christ our Lord. Amen.

• Father of mercies and God of all comfort, our only help in time of need and distress, we humbly beg you to relieve your sick servant for whom our prayers are offered. Look upon him (her) with your great mercy; comfort him (her) with a sense of your goodness; give him (her) patience in his (her) affliction. In your good time restore him (her) to health and enable him (her) to live the rest of his (her) life in your love and to your glory. Amen.

For One About to Undergo an Operation

• Heavenly Father, graciously comfort and encourage your servant in his (her) suffering and bless the means available for his (her) cure. Fill his (her) heart with absolute confidence in you and teach him (her) to put complete trust in your goodness and power. Through Jesus Christ our Lord. Amen.

For Childbirth

PRIEST: Our help is in the name of the Lord.

PEOPLE: Who made heaven and earth.

PRIEST: The Lord be with you.

PEOPLE: And also with you.

Let us pray.

• Our help is in the name of the Lord who made heaven and earth. O Lord, be a tower of strength to your servant N., and send her aid from your holy place. Almighty and everlasting God, Creator of all things, you who are mighty and awe-inspiring, just and merciful, you alone are kind and loving. By the co-working of the Holy Spirit, you prepared the body and soul of the Virgin Mary to become a worthy home for your Son. Receive the sacrifice of your servant N. who humbly asks you for the welfare of the child which you permitted her to conceive. May the hand of your mercy assist her delivery and may her child come to the light of day without harm, to serve you in all things and attain everlasting life. Through Christ, your Son and our Lord, who lives and reigns for ever and ever. Amen.

For the Poor and Neglected

PRIEST: Our help is in the name of the Lord.

PEOPLE: Who made heaven and earth.

PRIEST: The Lord be with you.

PEOPLE: And also with you.

Let us pray.

• Most merciful God, help us to remember all poor and neglected persons, whom it would be so easy to forget: the homeless, the destitute, the aged and the sick — particularly those who have no one to care for them. May your fatherly goodness rest upon them. Heal and comfort those who are broken in spirit and turn their sorrow into joy. Lift up the downhearted and cheer them with new hope. Keep them from being discouraged and help them from despairing. Grant this, our heavenly Father, for the love of your Son who, for our sake, became poor. Through Jesus Christ our Lord. Amen.

For Those Who Mourn or Are Bereaved

PRIEST: Our help is in the name of the Lord.

PEOPLE: Who made heaven and earth.

PRIEST: The Lord be with you.

PEOPLE: And also with you.

Let us pray.

• Almighty God, Father of mercies and giver of all comfort, look with pity on the sorrows of your afflicted servants. Remember them; nourish them with patience; comfort them with a sense of your goodness. Lift up their countenance as they cast their cares on you, so that they may know the genuine strength and consolation of your love. Amen.

• Give an abundance of faith and courage to all who mourn, that they may have the required strength to face the days ahead with steadfastness and patience — not sorrowing without hope, but in thankful remembrance of your great goodness and love in past years and a sure expectation of a joyful reunion with those they love. Amen.

Blessing in Time of Sorrow

PRIEST: Our help is in the name of the Lord.

PEOPLE: Who made heaven and earth.

PRIEST: The Lord be with you.

PEOPLE: And also with you.

Let us pray.

• Blessed are you, Lord God, ruler of all creation. We praise you for the gifts you have bestowed upon us. Help us in this time of sorrow and distress. Strengthen us, for we entrust our lives and all that we do into your hands, our heavenly Father. Amen.

For Families

PRIEST: Our help is in the name of the Lord.

PEOPLE: Who made heaven and earth.

PRIEST: The Lord be with you.

PEOPLE: And also with you.

Let us pray.

• O God our Father, bind our families together. Banish anger and destroy bitterness within them; nourish forgiveness among them and develop a strong sense of peace. Bestow upon parents such wisdom and patience that they may greatly exercise the spirit of genuine Christlike love and bring forth from their children their greatest virtues and the best that is in them. Instill in their children self-respect and right ideals, so that they may obey their parents and grow in their love and the joy of their companionship. Open ears to hear the truth another speaks; open eyes to see the reality beneath another's appearance, and make family affection reflect the genuine sign of Christ's love for all mankind. Amen.

Blessing of a House*

PRIEST: Our help is in the name of the Lord.

PEOPLE: Who made heaven and earth.

PRIEST: The Lord be with you.

PEOPLE: And also with you.

Let us pray.

Peace to this house, and to all who enter here.
Sprinkle me, O Lord, with blessed water, and I shall be purified; wash me and I shall be whiter than snow.

Have mercy on me, O God, in your great mercy. Glory be to the Father, and to the Son, and to the Holy Spirit. As it was in the beginning, is now, and ever shall be, world without end. Amen.

O Lord, hear my prayer and let my cry come to you. The Lord be with you and with your spirit.

(*Concluding prayer for any or all of these blessings.)

• Come, Lord God, we humbly beg you, and fill this house with the serenity of your love, joy and peace. Shower your benediction and grace in abundance upon all who dwell herein. May the peace and blessing of almighty God rest upon this house and all who dwell in it. Amen.

• Hear us, Lord, holy Father, almighty and eternal God, and graciously send your holy angel from heaven to watch over, to cherish, to protect, to abide with, and to defend all who dwell in this house. Through Christ our Lord. Amen.

• Lord, you are acquainted with all our ways, preserve all in this house in their going out and their coming in. Give ear, Lord, to their prayers and with your grace protect them; pour forth blessings upon both their bodies and souls, that they may serve you in this life and in the world to come. Amen.

• Blessed be your name, our God, our shelter from all that homelessness and lack of place can mean. Blessed be your name, for you have sheltered us. Bless now this house, this dwelling place of life and love, for you alone assure the peace and strength, the care that covers all our differences. You make these rooms a source of confidence, of dignity and freedom, for the members of our family household, and therefore for our country and the world. Let your Spirit dwell in us and open us to all who need our hospitality and care. Amen.

• O Lord God, you who have taught us that everything that we do, if not done in the spirit of charity and love, is worth nothing, give your blessing to this house, so that they who dwell therein may be knit together in true fellowship here upon earth and finally may be joined in the everlasting joy of heaven. Amen.

• O God, the Creator of all things, whose blessed Son worked in the carpenter shop of Nazareth, be present with those who work in this house and grant that, laboring as true Christians, they may share in the joy of your creation. Through Jesus Christ our Lord. Amen.

• O Lord, protect this house and let your holy angels dwell herein. May the Lord be with you always and remain ever with you. Heavenly Father, of whom the whole family in heaven and on earth is named, be present in this house, so that all who live here will be kindly disposed toward each other and may always find it a haven of blessing and peace. Through Jesus Christ our Lord. Amen.

Parental Blessing of a Child

PRIEST: Our help is in the name of the Lord.
PEOPLE: Who made heaven and earth.
PRIEST: The Lord be with you.
PEOPLE: And also with you.
Let us pray.

• Heavenly Father, bless N. and keep him (her) in your love and protection. Grant him (her) a good rest tonight [or a good day, a good journey, etc.] and send your angels to protect him (her). In the name of the Father, and of the Son, and of the Holy Spirit. Amen. *(The parent may make the sign of the cross on the child's forehead or simply lay his hands on the child's head in silence.)*

For Guidance

PRIEST: Our help is in the name of the Lord.
PEOPLE: Who made heaven and earth.
PRIEST: The Lord be with you.
PEOPLE: And also with you.
Let us pray.

• Direct us, O Lord, in everything that we do with your most gracious fervor and continual help. Teach us to begin, continue and end all of our work under your guidance, so that we constantly glorify your name and finally obtain eternal life. We ask this through Jesus Christ our Lord. Amen.

• Lord, guide our humble efforts to a right judgment in everything that we do, and dispel the ignorance of ungodly men by the light of your truth. In all our doubts, uncertainties and troubles, grant us your grace so that we may always seek your will and, being turned away from the ways of error, we may see the true light and be directed to you, Jesus Christ our Lord. Amen.

All Souls' Day and Memorial Day

PRIEST: Our help is in the name of the Lord.
PEOPLE: Who made heaven and earth.
PRIEST: The Lord be with you.
PEOPLE: And also with you.

Let us pray.

• Almighty and merciful God, remember our beloved dead, our family and friends, those who have laid down their lives in the service of our great country so that we may have and continue to esteem freedom, peace and happiness. Grant all of these your mercy and the light of your presence. May their deaths have not been in vain, but increase in all of us the desire and the will to work for justice and peace among all peoples and nations. This we ask in the name of Jesus Christ our Lord. Amen.

Blessing for a Good Harvest

PRIEST: Our help is in the name of the Lord.
PEOPLE: Who made heaven and earth.
PRIEST: The Lord be with you.
PEOPLE: And also with you.

Let us pray.

• There is a time to plant and a time to harvest, heavenly Father. Continue to bless, preserve and defend from every injury this harvest. We pray for an increase of the earth and the gathering of its fruits. Grant that we, having our desire for earthly needs fulfilled, may have a lively sense of your great mercy toward us, that we may serve you well, praise your goodness and mercy without ceasing and make such use of our temporal blessings so as not to lose our eternal goods. Through Christ our Lord. Amen.

Blessing of the Hunt

PRIEST: Our help is in the name of the Lord.
PEOPLE: Who made heaven and earth.

PRIEST: The Lord be with you.

PEOPLE: And also with you.

Let us pray.

• O God, our refuge and our strength, the source of all goodness, heed our prayers and grant that we fully obtain whatever we ask for in faith.

Almighty and everlasting God, you who helped the illustrious St. Anthony to emerge unscathed from the many temptations that beset him in this world, help us your servants to grow in virtue by his noble example.

Lord, bless the animals in this hunt to the benefit of their being, and by the intercession of St. Anthony deliver them from all and every evil. We ask this through Christ our Lord. Amen.

Blessing of Rosary Beads

PRIEST: Our help is in the name of the Lord.

PEOPLE: Who made heaven and earth.

PRIEST: The Lord be with you.

PEOPLE: And also with you.

Let us pray.

• For the praise and glory of the Blessed Virgin Mary, Mother of God, and in commemoration of the life of our Lord Jesus Christ, may these beads be blessed and sanctified in the name of the Father, and of the Son, and of the Holy Spirit. Amen.

Blessing of Articles of Devotion

PRIEST: Our help is in the name of the Lord.

PEOPLE: Who made heaven and earth.

PRIEST: The Lord be with you.

PEOPLE: And also with you.

Let us pray.

• Father in heaven, we praise you for sending your Spirit into our hearts to teach us to pray. Bless this (these) [name of article(s)], and teach us to use it (them) as an aid to sincere and devoted prayer. May we continue to grow in prayer and to please you by our lives. Grant that through it (them) we may increase your service for the good of all your people. All praise and glory be yours, heavenly Father. Amen.

A New Year's Blessing

PRIEST: Our help is in the name of the Lord.

PEOPLE: Who made heaven and earth.

PRIEST: The Lord be with you.

PEOPLE: And also with you.

Let us pray.

• All praise to you, Lord God, King of the universe: you have brought us to the beginning of a new year. Bless us and all that we do in your service, so that we may work for your honor and glory, and for the salvation of your people. Let us grow in love, patience and kindness and to maturity in Christ throughout this year. Father, we ask these things through Christ our Lord. Amen.

For an Automobile
(Or Any Other Kind of Vehicle)

PRIEST: Our help is in the name of the Lord.

PEOPLE: Who made heaven and earth.

PRIEST: The Lord be with you.

PEOPLE: And also with you.

Let us pray.

• O Lord God, listen favorably to our prayers, and bless this car [or truck, wagon, etc.]. Send your holy angels, so that all who ride in it may be delivered and guarded from every danger. And as you granted faith and grace to your deacon Philip, and to the man from Ethiopia who was sitting in his chariot and reading Holy Scripture, show the way of salvation to your servants, so that, helped by your grace and always intent on doing good works, they may, after all the trials of their pilgrimage and life on earth, attain to everlasting joy. Through Christ our Lord. Amen.

For Travelers

PRIEST: Our help is in the name of the Lord.

PEOPLE: Who made heaven and earth.

PRIEST: The Lord be with you.

PEOPLE: And also with you.

Let us pray.

• Heavenly Father, whose glory fills the entire creation and whose presence we find wherever we go, preserve those who travel and in particular those about to begin this journey. Surrounding them with your loving care, protect them from every danger and bring them back in safety to their journey's end. We ask this through Christ our Lord. Amen.

• Into the way of peace and prosperity, may the almighty and merciful Lord lead us, and may the Angel Raphael be with us on the way, that we may come to our home again in peace and health.

Save your servants, my God, who hope in you.

Lord, send us your help and strengthen us out of Sion.

Be unto us, O Lord, a tower of strength from the face of the enemy.

Let not the enemy prevail against us, nor the son of iniquity have power to harm us.

Blessed be the Lord daily and may the God of our salvation make our way prosperous.

Show us your ways, O Lord, and teach us your paths.

O Lord, hear our prayer and let our cry come unto you.

May your holy angel accompany us. Be unto us, O Lord, a help when we go forward, a comfort by the way, a shadow from the heat, a covering from the rain and the cold, a refuge in trouble.

Graciously hear our supplications, we beseech you, O Lord, and grant that your family may fare onward in the path of salvation, that this journey will teach all the great lesson of patience, brotherly love, kindness and gratitude for all the gifts bestowed on mankind by God the Father, God the Son, and God the Holy Spirit. Amen.

Travelers' Blessing

• Bless us in our travels. We praise you, O God, for this privilege of letting us admire these sights of nature — these mountains, these rivers, these lakes, these forests. We thank you for calling us to be your people, to admire and appreciate what you have given us. Help us to continue in your love and to praise you forever. Amen.

For Safe Travel

• Heavenly Father, we thank you for this journey safely ended and for the many persons who served or helped us on our trip. We thank you for your guiding hand, preserving us from dangers, seen and unseen along the way. We are grateful for the recreation and happiness it brought us. Grant that as a result we may lead better lives and will be drawn closer to you, the giver of all good gifts. Amen.

For Any Special Need

PRIEST: Our help is in the name of the Lord.

PEOPLE: Who made heaven and earth.

PRIEST: The Lord be with you.

PEOPLE: And also with you.

Let us pray.

• God our Father, our strength in adversity, our health in weakness, our comfort in sorrow, be merciful to all of us who implore your help. Listen to our prayers, receive the gifts we offer, look kindly on our sufferings, turn away from us your anger, and shower your love upon us. We ask this through Christ our Lord. Amen.

• Merciful God, deepen our faith in you as Creator and Father of all. Fill our hearts with a spirit of peace and reconciliation. Let us be your instruments of peace and making all things in Christ. May we grow strong in your image through which we can spread your message of love and peace in our own community and throughout the world. Grant this through your Son Jesus Christ, our Lord and Savior. Amen.

• Blessed are you, Father. Teach us to accept your holy will, and help us in our time of need. Praise to you, Lord God, Father of our Lord Jesus Christ. We thank you for all the many blessings you have bestowed upon us. Amen.

Blessing for All Things

PRIEST: Our help is in the name of the Lord.

PEOPLE: Who made heaven and earth.

PRIEST: The Lord be with you.

PEOPLE: And also with you.

Let us pray.

• O God, by whose word all things are made holy, pour down your blessing on this (these) [name of article(s)] which you created. Grant that whoever, giving thanks to you, uses it (them) in accordance with your law and your will, may, by calling upon your holy name, receive through your aid health of body and protection of soul. Through Christ our Lord. Amen.

General Blessing

PRIEST: Our help is in the name of the Lord.

PEOPLE: Who made heaven and earth.

PRIEST: The Lord be with you.

PEOPLE: And also with you.

Let us pray.

• O Father, listen to our prayer,
And guard your family with your care.
We pause amid our work to pray,
And ask your blessing throughout this day.
Upon your Church your graces pour:
Protect us now and evermore.
Deliver us from sin and sloth,
And aid us in your Spirit's growth.
May peace be given to all lands,
And food to all with empty hands.
May all our words be for your praise,
And lead us in salvation's ways.
O Father, may our work for you
Rebuild your Church and make it new.
We honor Son and Spirit, too:
All glory, honor, praise to you. Amen.

Prayer for Authorities*
(Traditionally Recited on Thanksgiving Day)

PRIEST: Our help is in the name of the Lord.

PEOPLE: Who made heaven and earth.

PRIEST: The Lord be with you.

PEOPLE: And also with you.

Let us pray.

• We ask you, almighty and eternal God, who through Jesus Christ has revealed your glory to all the nations, that your Church, being spread throughout the whole world, may continue, with unchanging faith, in the confession of your name. We pray, O Lord — through whom authority is rightly administered, laws are enacted and judgment decreed — that you assist the President of the United States in his administration, that it may be conducted in righteousness, and that it may be eminently useful to your people, over whom he presides, by encouraging due respect for virtue and religion; by faithfully executing the nation's laws in justice and mercy; and by restraining vice and immorality. Let the light of your divine wisdom direct the deliberations of congress, and let it shine forth in all the proceedings and laws framed

---

*Based on a prayer composed by Archbishop John Carroll.

for our rule and government, so that they may tend to the preservation of peace, the promotion of national happiness, the increase of industry, sobriety and useful knowledge, and the perpetuation to us of the blessings of equal liberty. Amen.

For Peace Among Nations

PRIEST: Our help is in the name of the Lord.

PEOPLE: Who made heaven and earth.

PRIEST: The Lord be with you.

PEOPLE: And also with you.

Let us pray.

• Almighty God, the Father of all men upon earth, most heartily we pray that you will keep your people from the cruelties of war, and lead all nations in the way of peace. Teach us to put away all bitterness and misunderstanding, so that we, with all our brethren, may be drawn together as one people and dwell evermore in the fellowship of the Prince of peace, who lives and reigns for ever and ever. Amen.

• Almighty, ever-living God, it is you we praise for our nation's years of life and growth. It is to your word we owe the founding fathers' vision of liberty and justice for all. Make this our vision and our constant goal. Out of many nations, many people, you have made us one, though we are not yet one in our own hearts and deeds. May your Spirit heal all of our divisions and disunity. Help us to respect and prize and share with full acceptance the rich, various and different gifts of this great people, that we may work together for a common good. Amen.

• Almighty, ever-living God, you alone are Lord. Before you, we and all our institutions, our nation and our government are modest creatures, bound by human limits, possessing fragile power. We give you thanks and praise you for our years as a nation, for the gifts of this land's native people, for the vision and aspiration of the founders, for people from many countries who have here found a home and cherished liberty. Let your Spirit purify our love of country that it may be true, that it may face the evil in us without being diminished, caring for all that is good in our heritage, striving for all that is possible in our future. Heal the wounds that injustice, past and present, has inflicted. Lay low the barriers that it has built. Move us to find ways of sharing the resources of the world as sisters and as brothers, with liberty and justice for all people. Through Christ our Lord. Amen.

• God of all gifts, blessings we cannot remember, blessings we

231

sometimes hardly sense: you have made us a people; you have given us a place. We praise you for everything that is true and beautiful about this nation, its places and its people. It is beyond our power to thank you fully, Father, for our rich variety of people and for nature's abundant gifts. We can only exclaim our wonder, our joy, our feelings about the poverty that we would suffer if it were not so. It is right to give you thanks and praise. Amen.

INDEX

Absolution, general — 42ff
Abstinence, fast and — 32
Admission of other Christians to Eucharistic Communion in a Catholic Church — 25f
Adoration during exposition of the Blessed Sacrament — 29f
Alcoholic priests — 25
All Souls' Day — 21f
All Souls' Day and Memorial Day, prayer for — 225
Altar — 19
       Adornment of — 20
       Incensation of — 35f
Anniversary, celebration of wedding — 97f
Anointing, rite of — 145ff
       Commentary on, pastoral — 145ff
       Guidelines for — 148f
Anointing of the sick, sacrament of — 148f
Antiphon, final, of the Virgin Mary — 31
Armed forces, prayer for those in — 218f
Articles of devotion, blessing of — 226
Authorities, civil, prayer for — 217
Authorities (Thanksgiving Day), prayer for — 230
Automobile (or any other vehicle), blessing for — 227
"Ave Verum" — 132

Banners, church — 31f
Baptism, celebration of — 39f
Benediction and exposition of the Blessed Sacrament, rite of — 127ff
Bereaved or mourners, prayers for — 221f
Bination on weekdays — 21
Blessed Sacrament, exposition of — 125ff
Blessing
       For an automobile (or any other vehicle) — 227
       For an elderly person — 219
       For a good harvest — 225
       For the New Year — 227
       General — 229f
       In time of sorrow — 222
       Of articles of devotion — 226
       Of a child, parental — 224
       Of a house — 223f
       Of the hunt — 225f
       Of love (St. Francis) — 211f
       Of rosary beads — 226
       Of a school — 219
       Of travelers — 227f
Blessings for persons, places and things — 211ff

Bread and wine — 20
Burial services — 171ff
    Final commendation and farewell in church after Mass — 190ff
    Final commendation and farewell when omitted in church —
    199ff
    Funeral Mass, preparations for church and cemetery — 174
    Homilies, funeral — 179f
        For a child — 184f
        For an elderly person — 185f
        For a public servant — 182f
        General — 176ff
    Law of the Code — 189
    Public celebration of Mass for deceased separated Christians —
    187ff
    Vigil service on the eve of burial — 171ff

Canon Law — 13ff, 187ff and *passim*
Catechists — 75f and *passim*
Celebration of Mass — 24 and *passim*
Celebration of confirmation, offices and ministries in — 73
Chair, celebrant's — 19
Childbirth, prayer for — 221
Child, funeral homily for — 184f
Child, parental blessing of — 224
Choir and organ — 19
Church, prayers for — 215f
Church unity, prayer for — 216
Code of Canon Law — 13ff, 187ff and *passim*
Commendation and farewell, final, in church after Mass — 190ff
Commendation and farewell, final, when omitted in church — 199ff
Commentator-lector and song leader for confirmation — 77f
Communal penance services — 48ff
Communion
    Under both kinds — 20
    Distribution of — 24
Concelebration — 21
Confessional room, rite of reconciliation — 31
Confirmation
    Catechists — 75f
    Commentator-lector and song leader for — 77f
    Liturgical considerations of — 74f
    Music appendix for — 84f
    Order of rite of — 79ff
        Outside the Mass — 84
    Sacrament of — 73ff
        Ceremony of — 74
        Dignity of — 73
        Liturgical reform — 73
        Offices and ministries in the celebration of — 73f

Confirmation administered by a priest — 27f
Congress or a state legislature, prayers for — 217f
Country, prayer for — 216f
Cremation and Christian burial — 207ff

Danger of death, prayers for persons in — 142f
Deacon, role of — 18
Dignity of confirmation — 73
Distribution of Holy Communion — 24
Dying, prayers for — 151ff

Easter vigil — 28f and *passim*
Eastern Rites — 14 and *passim*
Elderly and infirm priests — 25
Enemies, prayer for our — 215
Eucharist
     Admission of other Christians to — 25ff
     Distribution of — 24
     Extraordinary ministers of — 34f
     Fasting for — 23f
     On Good Friday — 28
     Receiving twice on same day — 30f, 34
     Reservation of — 19
Eucharistic
     Congress prayer — 136
     Day or Holy Hour — 136
Exhortation before matrimony — 88ff
Exposition of the Blessed Sacrament — 29f
     Eucharistic Congress prayer — 136
     Eucharistic day or Holy Hour — 136
     Exposition and Mass relationship — 125
     Hymns — 130ff
     Litany of the Sacred Heart — 135f
     Meditation and prayers — 133f
     Minister of — 127
     Regulations for — 125ff
     Rite of, exposition and benediction of the Blessed Sacrament — 127ff
          Reposition of — 130
     Scripture readings, suggested — 136f
Extraordinary ministers of the Eucharist — 34
Eye disorders, prayers for patients with — 141f

Families, prayer for — 222
Fast and abstinence, Lenten — 32
Fast, Eucharistic — 23f
Fellowmen, prayers for our — 213f
First Communion — 30
Folk Mass — 19
Forgiveness, essay on — 71f

Funeral homilies — *See* Homilies, funeral
Funeral Mass, preparations for church and cemetery — 174
Funeral of non-Catholics — 35

General blessing — 229f
Good Friday — 28
Grace at meals — 214
Guidance, prayers for — 224f

Harvest, good, blessing for — 225
Holy Communion, distribution of — 24
Holy Eucharist — *See* Eucharist
Holy Thursday — 28
Homily — 17 and *passim*
    Sign of the cross — 18
Homilies for matrimony — 90ff
Homilies, funeral — 171ff
    For a child — 184f
    For an elderly person — 185f
    For a public servant — 182f
    General — 176ff
Hour of Mass — 23
House, blessing of — 223f
Hunt, blessing of — 225f
Hymns (Blessed Sacrament) — 130ff

Immersion (baptismal rite) — 39
Incensation — 35
    Of the altar — 35
Infusion (baptismal rite) — 39
Intercessions, general, for marriage ceremony — 104ff
Intercommunion
    Catholics in Orthodox Churches — 26
    Catholics in Protestant Churches — 26
    Orthodox in Catholic Churches — 26
    Protestants in Catholic Churches — 26
Intinction, Holy Communion by — 21

Kiss (or sign) of peace — 36f

Law, liturgical — 13ff and *passim*
Lectern — 19
Linens, sacred, washing of — 32
Litany of the Sacred Heart — 135f
Liturgical considerations of confirmation — 74f
Liturgical law — *See* Law, liturgical

Marian penance service — 58ff
Marriage ceremony with Mass, preparations for — 87

Marriage ceremony without Mass, preparations for — 87
Mass
    All Souls' Day — 21f
    Bination on weekdays — 21
    Celebration of — 24
    Concelebration — 21 and *passim*
    Folk — 19
    Holy Thursday — 28
    Homes, in — 23
    Hour of — 23
    Language — 17
    Place of — 25
    Pro populo — 24
    Public celebration of, for deceased separated Christians — 187ff
    Sine populo — 17
    Stipends — 24
    Sunday vigil — 22f
    Time of — 23
    Trination — 22
    Vigil of Easter — 28f
Mass and exposition, relationship — 125
Mass, funeral, preparations for church and cemetery — 174
Mass in homes — 23
Mass, public, for deceased separated Christians — 187ff
Matrimony
    Anniversary celebration — 97f
    Exhortation before ceremony — 88f
    Homilies for ceremony — 90ff
    Intercessions for ceremony — 104ff
    Mixed marriage guidelines — 119ff
    Prayer of bride and bridegroom, suggested, after Communion — 113f
    Preparations for ceremony with Mass — 87
    Preparations for ceremony without Mass — 87
    Reading before ceremony — 87f
    Renewal of vows — 98
    Rite for celebrating during Mass — 99ff
    Rite for celebrating outside Mass — 114ff
    Sacrament of — 87ff
Meals, grace at — 214
Meditation and prayers — 133f
Minister of exposition — 127
Ministers, extraordinary, of the Eucharist — 34f
Missa pro populo — 24
Mixed marriage guidelines — 119ff
Music appendix for confirmation — 84f

Need, special, prayers for — 229
New Year's blessing — 227

Offices and ministries in the celebration of confirmation — 73f

Operation, prayer for one about to undergo — 220
Organ and choir — 19
Oriental Catholics — 27
"O Sacrum Convivium" — 132

"Pange Lingua" — 130f
Peace, prayers for — 212
Peace among nations, prayers for — 231f
Peace, sign (or kiss) of — 36f
Penance, communal
     Appendix of scriptural texts for — 65ff
     General outline for — 45
     Guidelines for — 45f
     Marian penance service — 58ff
     Services for — 48ff, 52ff
     Texts, optional for — 46ff
Penitential rite — 80
Person, elderly, blessing for — 219
Place of Mass — 25
Poor and neglected, prayer for — 221
Prayers
     For All Souls' Day and Memorial Day — 225
     For authorities (Thanksgiving Day) — 230f
     For childbirth — 221
     For civil authorities — 217
     For the Church — 215f
     For Church unity — 216
     For congress or a state legislature — 217f
     For the dying — 151ff
     For families — 222
     For guidance — 224f
     For mourners or the bereaved — 221f
     For one about to undergo an operation — 220
     For our country — 216f
     For our enemies — 215
     For our fellowmen — 213f
     For peace — 212
     For peace among nations — 231f
     For the poor and neglected — 221
     For safe travel — 228
     For schools and colleges — 219
     For the sick — 220
     For social justice — 218
     For special need — 229
     For Thanksgiving Day — 215
     For those in the armed forces — 218f
     For those in danger of death — 142f
     For those with eye disorders — 141f
     For travelers — 227f
     Of thanksgiving — 212f

Prayers — *continued*

    Traditional
        Act of contrition — 143f
        Act of faith — 143
        Act of hope — 143
        Act of love — 143
        Act of resignation to death — 144
    When visiting the sick — 139ff
Prayer of bride and bridegroom, suggested, after Communion — 113f
Preaching — 17 and *passim*
Priests
    Alcoholic — 25
    Elderly and infirm — 25
Pro populo, Mass — 24
Public celebration of Mass for deceased separated Christians — 187ff
Public servant, funeral homily for — 182f

Reading before marriage ceremony — 87f
Reception of baptized Christians — 32f
Reconciliation, sacrament of — 41ff
    Absolution, general — 42f
    Dress, proper — 43
    Minister, competent — 41
    Parts, essential — 41
    Penance, communal, outline for — 45
    Place — 41
    Time — 41
Reform, liturgical — 73
Renewal of marriage vows — 98
Reposition of Blessed Sacrament — 125
Reservation of the Eucharist — 19
Rite for celebrating marriage during the Mass — 99ff
Rite for celebrating marriage outside the Mass — 114ff
Rite of confirmation, order of — 79ff
    Outside the Mass — 84
Rite of Eucharistic exposition and benediction — 127ff
Role of the deacon — 18
Rosary beads, blessing of — 226
Rubrics, essential and accidental — 15f

Sacrament
    Of anointing — 33, 145ff
    Of baptism — 39ff
    Of confirmation — 73ff
    Of matrimony — 87ff
    Of reconciliation — 41ff
Sacramentary — 16 and *passim*
Sacred Heart, litany of — 135f
Sacrifice of the Mass — *See* Mass
Sacristan and master of ceremonies for confirmation, notes for — 77

Safe travel, prayer for — 228
Schillebeeckx, Edward (*Mary, Mother of the Redemption*) — 65
School, blessing of — 219
Schools and colleges, prayer for — 219
Scriptural texts for communal penance service, appendix of — 65ff
Services for communal penance — 48ff
        Appendix of scriptural texts for — 65ff
        Marian penance service — 58ff
Sick, prayers for — 220
Sick, prayers when visiting — 139ff
Sign of the cross — 18 and *passim*
Sign (or kiss) of peace — 36f
Sine populo, Mass — 17
Special need, prayer for — 229
Stipends — 24
Sunday obligation on Saturday, fulfilling — 22f

"Tantum Ergo" — 131f
Texts, optional, for communal penance — 46
        Scriptural texts, appendix of — 65ff
Texts, scriptural, alternate, for wake services — 164ff
Thanksgiving Day, special prayer for — 215
Thanksgiving, prayers of — 212f
Things, all, blessing for — 229
Time of Mass — 25
Travelers, prayer for — 227f
Travelers' blessing — 228
Trination — 22
Twice on same day, receiving Holy Communion — 30, 34

Vessels, sacred — 20
Viaticum — 24 and *passim*
Vigil of Easter, Mass on — 28f
Vigil service on the eve of burial — 171ff
Visiting the sick, prayers when — 139ff

Wake services — 159ff
        Scriptural texts, alternate for — 164ff
Washing of sacred linens — 32
Wedding banquet, grace before — 215
Wine and bread — 20